D0249420

claiming
your place
at the fire

RICHARD J. LEIDER
DAVID A. SHAPIRO

claiming
your place
at the fire

LIVING THE SECOND
HALF OF YOUR LIFE
ON PURPOSE

BERRETT-KOEHLER PUBLISHERS, INC.
San Francisco

Copyright © 2004. Richard J. Leider and David A. Shapiro

All rights reserved. No part of this publication may be reproduced, distributed, or transmitted in any form or by any means, including photocopying, recording, or other electronic or mechanical methods, without the prior written permission of the publisher, except in the case of brief quotations embodied in critical reviews and certain other noncommercial uses permitted by copyright law. For permission requests, write to the publisher, addressed "Attention: Permissions Coordinator," at the address below.

Berrett-Koehler Publishers, Inc.
235 Montgomery Street, Suite 650
San Francisco, CA 94104-2916
Tel: (415) 288-0260   Fax: (415) 362-2512   www.bkconnection.com

Ordering Information
Quantity sales. Special discounts are available on quantity purchases by corporations, associations, and others. For details, contact the "Special Sales Department" at the Berrett-Koehler address above.
Individual sales. Berrett-Koehler publications are available through most bookstores. They can also be ordered direct from Berrett-Koehler: Tel: (800) 929-2929;
Fax: (802) 864-7626; www.bkconnection.com
Orders for college textbook/course adoption use. Please contact Berrett-Koehler:
Tel: (800) 929-2929; Fax: (802) 864-7626.
Orders by U.S. trade bookstores and wholesalers. Please contact Publishers Group West, 1700 Fourth Street, Berkeley, CA 94710. Tel: (510) 528-1444; Fax (510) 528-3444.
Berrett-Koehler and the BK logo are registered trademarks of Berrett-Koehler Publishers, Inc.

Printed in the United States of America

Berrett-Koehler books are printed on long-lasting acid-free paper. When it is available, we choose paper that has been manufactured by environmentally responsible processes. These may include using trees grown in sustainable forests, incorporating recycled paper, minimizing chlorine in bleaching, or recycling the energy produced at the paper mill.

Library of Congress Cataloging-in-Publication Data
Leider, Richard.
   Claiming your place at the fire : living the second half of your life on purpose / Richard J. Leider, David A. Shapiro.
        p. cm.
   Includes index.
   ISBN 1-57675-297-6
   1. Older people—Conduct of life. I. Shapiro, David A., 1957–. II. Title
BJ1691.L42 2004
158.1′084′4—dc22   2004047786

FIRST EDITION

09 08 07 06 05 04   10 9 8 7 6 5 4 3 2 1

Text design by Detta Penna
Copyediting by Patricia Brewer

Contents

Invitation to the Fire

If we were to describe our lives using the metaphor of fire, we would recognize that there comes a time when the flames have settled into a comfortable glow. The fire is steady, burning warmly, and in no danger of going out anytime soon. There is plenty of fuel to add to it, but no rush to do so. A bank of coals lies at the base of the fire, white hot and powerful. The fire has been well tended and is now ready to give back great heat and light for some time to come.

This is a book for people who are moving into and through the stage of life characterized by that fire. It is for people who are ready to stoke the wisdom gained in the first half of their lives to burn with a brighter sense of purpose in the second half.

The book presents a new model of vital aging for people entering into and moving through the second half of their lives. We want to emphasize the "growing" aspect of growing older and highlight the ways in which we ascend, rather than descend, in the second half of life. In doing so, we aim to retire the concept of retirement as it is seen today.

To claim one's place at the fire means to live one's life on purpose. When we claim our place at the fire, we enter into the circle of vital elders who have been the source of wisdom in society since time immemorial. We do this by courageously reexamining and rediscovering who we are, where we belong, what we care about, and what our life's purpose is.

We believe that the second half of life offers us unique opportunities for growing whole, not old. When we claim our place at the fire—by recalling our stories, refinding our place, renewing our calling, and reclaiming our purpose—we ultimately embrace the deepest expression of who we really are.

And so, we invite you to join us at the fire to explore how to become "new elders." It is time for those of us in the second half of life to look beyond simply defining ourselves as old. We know we are old. New elders accept this and yet continue to actively seek new life and vitality. And so, it is our hope that what follows can provide you with a vital new model of aging and retirement for you, your loved ones, and for the world we share together.

Richard J. Leider
Minneapolis, MN

David A. Shapiro
Seattle, WA

At the Fireside

The New Elder

This story begins where so many of the greatest stories ever told begin: around a blazing fire, beneath the starry heavens, far from civilization, deep in the wild. Richard recalls it this way:

On my twentieth walking safari in Tanzania, I find myself with my team of "inventurers"—our term for individuals who adventure inward through outdoor experience—sitting around the fire late into the evening with a small group of Hadza elders.

The Hadza are a tribe of hunter-gatherers who live today as did our earliest human ancestors. The ancient is present for them in this most elemental of human experiences. Gathered about a fire in an abundant region on the edge of a primeval baobab tree forest, they are grounded in the deepest sense with the natural world, their survival dependent upon it.

The elders of the tribe, in keeping with ancient tradition, sit closer to the fire. Younger members form a larger circle around them. Our inventure team is honored to sit among the elders. In the glow of the firelight, I see expressions of respect and deference on the faces of our group as we lean forward to take in the words of wisdom being shared with us.

The man who is speaking is named Maroba. He is a Hadza elder, deeply immersed in the ancient ways and stories of his people. Though barely five feet tall, Maroba exudes a solidity and power that belies his small stature.

He is sharing with us a story passed down from his parents and grandparents, from their parents and grandparents, from time immemorial. It is a story with a lesson that Maroba and his people understand in their very bones, and one that resonates powerfully across space and time

We call the story "The Gift of the Honey Guide," for the story itself is a gift, passed on from generation to generation and to us.

The Honey Guide is a small gray- and rust-colored bird, about the size of a robin, that flutters from branch to branch on the mighty baobab and acacia trees in the Hadza homeland.

Maroba tells us that from his youngest days he was taught that the Honey Guide is the friend of his people. He is the "indicator" bird, who points the way to life's sweetness. The Honey Guide indicates where to find the honey on which our lives depend, the honey that we need to survive.

We are reminded, says Maroba, to keep our eyes and ears open for the Honey Guide wherever we go. Should we hear the "weet-terr, weet-terr" of this wise bird, we must whistle back to let him know we are listening.

The Honey Guide will then fly close to us and flash his white tail feathers to get our attention. Follow him, whistling to him as he sings back, "weet-terr, weet-terr," and he will lead us to a bees' nest dripping with honey. We must then climb the tree and smoke out the bees and take the honeycomb.

Then here is the most important part of all, Maroba instructs: Before we eat the honey ourselves, we must break off a piece of the honeycomb and leave it for the Honey Guide to thank him for his guidance. Tribal wisdom has it that if we do not do so, he will no longer sing to us. Or worse, he may even play tricks on us, like choosing to sing when we are hunting, giving us away to the prey we are stalking.

Listening to Maroba's story with rapt attention, we know firsthand that it is not a myth. In fact, we know that it is true. Our group of 'inventurers' has seen the Honey Guide firsthand. We have witnessed with our own eyes and ears this amazing interaction between human beings and nature—a relationship that benefits both species involved.

Maroba's story calls us back to that miracle we have seen and reminds us that what we need in life is available to us if only we know how to look for it. And if only we remember that getting what really matters in life depends above all on giving it back.

At the end of the story, I lament that the torch of wisdom, and the legends like Maroba's, are not being passed through the generations in my world. I ask our team, "Do you have elders, like Maroba, who guide you?" Many reply sadly, "I don't know. No matter whom I think of, their role seems narrow or fragmented. I don't think we have real elders anymore."

As we stare into the glowing, late-night coals of the fire, Maroba asks me, "Who are the elders of your tribe?"

I try to answer but am stumped. I draw a blank. My "tribe"? What is that? My elders? Who are they? I cannot come up with a clear answer. The very concept of "elder" for our tribe—contemporary men and women in Western industrialized society—seems foreign. And yet it is clear to me that Maroba's question begs for an answer.

The next day, and as our trek wears on, Maroba's question— Who are the elders of your tribe?—stays with me and with our fireside conversations. We discuss it at length and come away with some answers, but many more questions.

Each night, sitting around another fire, our conversations dig deeper into what it means for us to be a wise elder. Clearly it is different than the traditional picture painted by Maroba, although many features are similar.

Perhaps most importantly, the idea of elder, for us, is distinct from being old. Those of us who aspire to being elders in our communities know that we are older; what is most important to us is a sense of vitality and purpose, a sense that we still matter and can make a difference in our own lives and in the lives of those around us. We aspire to a purposeful sense of self in elderhood.

We live in a culture that celebrates youth. Many mid-lifers, being members of—or close to—the baby boom generation, have been among those who have celebrated youth most enthusiastically. Now, though, finding ourselves no longer young—chronologically—we wonder about this emphasis on all that is new and fresh. We wonder about our place in the world and all that we have to offer as a result of our life experience.

Much of our fireside discussion comes back again and again to picturing the traditional setting of elders and tribal groups around the fire. The place of respect that elders are accorded in such settings represents a sharp contrast to how older adults in our society are often seen.

What strikes us vividly about this is the degree to which the elders in traditional societies earn and accept the respect they are given. It's not just that they are acknowledged by their people; that is a given. As importantly, they claim themselves as vital resources for their communities. Becoming an elder is, for them, an active step that involves staking out a place of power that one has achieved. We see this represented clearly by the place taken around the traditional fire. A person closest to the flames has to have something valuable to bring forth and must take the initiative to do so. In this way, he or she claims that place of respect at the fire.

This idea of "claiming" one's place at the fire illuminates our discussions. We see this step of owning our power as the missing piece to the role of elders in our society. We recognize that, at least to some degree, we have accepted our culture's picture of aging. We realize it is time for us—individually and as a group of people in the second half of our lives—to create a new picture of vital aging. It is time to claim our own places at the fire.

A new language emerges from our discussions. We begin calling ourselves the "new elders." New elders are people who use the second half of life as an empty canvas, a blank page, a hunk of clay to be crafted on purpose. These are people who never stop reinventing themselves.

For new elders, the past predicts but does not determine the future. New elders live the second half of their lives in ways characterized by an aliveness and vitality that is grounded in a deep sense of purpose and a refusal to—in the words of Dylan Thomas—"go gentle into that good night" as did many of their forebears.

For a world-renowned example of new elders at work in the world, we think of Jimmy and Rosalynn Carter. By teaching Sunday school, building low-cost homes for Habitat for Humanity, and working for reconciliation in fledgling democracies, the Carters have committed themselves to continual reinvention through giving and growing. They are putting to use the deep wisdom they have developed over their long and useful lives. They are experiencing a sense of liberation that only comes to us when we have discovered who we truly are and how best to express that.

Late one night, sitting alone, gazing into the firelight, I have an experience that seems to bring it all together. It is an odd and almost mystical experience, no doubt informed by the setting in which it takes place: a starlit night in an African baobab forest, the fire burning brightly. Around me, just beyond the firelight, the eyes of many animals wink on and off in the surrounding darkness.

As I stare into the fire, I reflect on four questions that, in our ongoing discussions of new elderhood, we have pondered at length:

Who am I? Where do I belong? What do I care about? And what is my life's purpose? The answers to these questions, though elusive, seem key to becoming a new elder. If we could only answer these questions, we would each discover new ways to become the new elder we aspire to be.

Staring into the fire, I suddenly see not just one flame, but four: four flames, one for each of the four questions.

The first is the flame of identity—who am I? It is the flame of our life's stories. Recalling our story is the means by which we rediscover and reinvent ourselves in the second half of life.

The second flame is the flame of community—where do I belong? It is the flame of our place. Refinding our place in the world is the means by which we embrace a sense of intimacy for the second half of life.

The third flame is the flame of passion—what do I care about? Renewing our life's calling is the means by which we stay connected to the world and mentor those who will see to things after we are gone.

And the fourth flame is the flame of meaning—why am I here? This is the flame that illuminates our life's purpose. Reclaiming our purpose is the means by which we find creative expression and make a difference in the lives of those around us.

The four flames are not utterly distinct from one another. They dance together in pairs, in trios, and as one. And yet, as I watch them, I begin to sense a framework for addressing the questions that must be answered should we aspire to become new elders.

And so from that fire, this book has emerged. This book is about living on purpose in the second half of life.

In the second half, the reward for surviving is the freedom to become yourself.

It is to answer Maroba's question: Who are the elders of our tribe?

We are . . . if only, like Maroba, we claim our place at the fire.

The Four Flames of Vital Aging

Living on Purpose in the Second Half of Life

In our earlier book, *Repacking Your Bags: Lighten Your Load for the Rest of Your Life,* we developed a definition of the "good life" that included four components: place, people, work, and purpose. We defined the good life as "Living in the place you belong, with people you love, doing the right work, on purpose." While this definition applied to people who were in the first half of their lives, we've found it to be no less pertinent to individuals who are entering into the second half.

In the second half of life, the same questions that drive our conception of the good life during the first half inevitably return. *Who am I? Where do I belong? What do I care about? What is my life's purpose?* Only now, in the second half, we have a unique opportunity to be the author of our own story. We have a chance to rewrite it, rather than simply replicate the first half.

It has become clear to us that becoming a new elder demands a rekindling of the good life. It requires drawing upon the wisdom we have gained in the first half.

With the four components of the good life in mind, we have been able to identify four common principles among those seasoned citizens who are becoming new elders—individuals who are living on purpose in the second half of their lives.

These principles have become apparent as we've observed the indicators around us. Unfortunately, unlike the Hadza, we have no Honey Guide to guide us. We have had, however, the good fortune to witness dozens of new elders—our own Honey Guides—in action. Their choices, behaviors, and ways of moving through the world have enabled us to identify the "four flames of vital aging"—the key components of a life lived on purpose during the second half.

These new elders have *rekindled* the good life for the second half. They have stoked the fire within and are sharing its warmth and light with others.

This fire metaphor does not arise by accident. It emerges naturally out of an ongoing exploration of what it means to be truly human. After all, nothing is more essential to the human experience than the experience of fire. Fire connects us to the deepest core of our shared humanity. Our most distant ancestors depended upon fire for their survival; our most distant descendents, like us, will employ fire in some form in order to live. The use of fire is quite literally what separates human beings from non-human beings. It is this understanding of the vital role that fire plays in our humanity that has given rise to the myths and stories of fire among indigenous peoples.

One of the most common ways that we talk about vitality is in terms of "keeping the fire alive." For this reason—as well as for the abiding role fire plays in linking past, present, and future—the fire theme naturally emerges in our story of new elders. Each of the four key principles of new elders is embodied in a characteristic of fire. In claiming our place at the fire as new elders, we claim each of these aspects ourselves.

1. The Flame of Identity: *Recalling Our Stories*

   Principle: *Wisdom*

   Firestarter Question: *Who Am I?*

   New elders harvest and transfer the wisdom of the past into the present. They know the important narratives of their culture, whatever that culture is. Joseph Campbell said, "The first requirement of any society is that its adult membership should realize and represent the fact it is they who constitute its life and being . . . and on which that society itself must depend for its existence." Elders teach by story. But it isn't simply recalling stories about "the good old days." Rather, it is an ability to touch the lives and lived experience of others through their own experiences in a manner that brings it alive in the present, through the past.

2. The Flame of Community: *Refinding Our Place*

   Principle: *Intimacy*

   Firestarter Question: *Where Do I Belong?*

   New elders know where they belong in the world; they have a powerful sense of place—where they have come from, where they are, and where they are going.

   Consequently, they are able to reaffirm who they are for the journey ahead; grounded in the rich history of their first half, they feel alive to the challenges of the second half.

3. The Flame of Passion: *Renewing Our Calling*

   Principle: *Caring*

   Firestarter Question: *What Do I Care About?*

   Perhaps no challenge is greater for people in the second half of life than to find something meaningful and valuable to do with their gifts. New elders consistently meet that challenge by applying their gifts in support of young people and the community at large. New elders care passionately about those who follow in their footsteps. They find deep satisfaction in giving their gifts in new ways that serve others rather than just themselves. And they accept this as a critical responsibility of their elderhood. Consequently, new elders are all about "giving it away." They know that a person is strong not in proportion to what he or she can hold on to, but rather, according to what the person can give up. This doesn't necessarily mean they are free-spending philanthropists when it comes to money; it does, however, usually mean they are extremely generous with advice, counsel, and support. While elders may hold important positions in life, they realize that real power stems from the willingness and ability to share it with others. They see wisdom as something that is inherent within everyone and, like the ancient philosopher Socrates, are passionate about helping to inspire that depth of wisdom within those around them.

4. The Flame of Meaning: *Reclaiming Our Purpose*

Principle: *Meaning*

Firestarter Question: *What Is My Legacy?*

New elders know "why they get up in the morning," and it isn't just because their alarm clock goes off. As a matter of fact, for many new elders, the alarm that dragged them out of bed for so many years has been permanently retired. Freed up from imposed schedules, they now find the freedom to make their own. And with that freedom, they are enthusiastically greeting the day, fired up about all they can do at last. These new elders burn with the beacon that guides them: their purpose. They light the way for themselves and for others to follow. The incandescence of such elders is powerfully illuminating. As they forge ahead, lit by the fire of purpose, they light the way into the future.

The four flames of vital aging represent choices available to all of us. We can make those choices no matter what age or stage we are in life. And while they are no doubt choices that lend themselves more naturally to those of us in the second half of life, new elders are by no means the elderly. In fact, as we may realize, it is often aging, or the fear of it, that prevents many of us from ever really becoming elders.

Now, more than ever, we need new elders among us. New elders are natural resources that are needed today by the family, the community, the organization, and the Earth. We can't wait for the wise ones to come. We need to become the new elders. It is incumbent upon us to accept the mantle of becoming new elders for ourselves, our loved ones, and the planet as a whole.

Stepping into the Elder Circle

In his powerful account of age and aging, Ram Dass discusses an activity called an Elder Circle, which he does with people in the second half of life to help them appreciate their power and wisdom. Employing a form common to traditional cultures, he invites the oldest members of groups he brings together to sit in the inner circle and share their wisdom with the younger members, who sit around them in an outer circle. He reports that many of the elders who take part in this exercise say that it is the first time their wisdom has ever been appreciated. In Ram Dass's words, "Because it does not know what to do with older people, our society has become impoverished of precisely those qualities its elders could offer. Unfortunately, most elders don't know, themselves, what it is they have to offer."

Our intention in this book is similar to what Ram Dass does in that exercise. We hope to provide you with a framework for coming to respect and appreciate your own power— a power of purpose that grows with age.

To claim one's power as a new elder, a certain amount of reflection upon the past is necessary. The lessons learned in the first half of life must be revisited and reapplied to the second half. This book is structured to help you do that.

In the next chapter, *The Flame of Identity: Recalling Our Stories,* we explore the guidance that the power of narrative gives us as we wonder "Who Am I?" As we are becoming new elders, it is incumbent upon us to harvest the wisdom we have gained during the first half of life in order to sow its seeds for the second half. Recalling the stories that make us (and which have made us) who we are sets the context for connecting and reconnecting with friends, family, and community members. We are thus better positioned to expand upon and share our wisdom with others as new elders.

Chapter 2, *The Flame of Community: Refinding Our Place,* addresses the question "Where Do I Belong?" Becoming a new elder offers us a unique opportunity for reexamining our place in the world. This chapter guides us by helping us to wonder what makes a place "home" and what we can do to create a sense of sacred space for the second half of life.

Chapter 3, *The Flame of Passion: Renewing Our Calling,* is a guide to the "What Do I Care About?" question. We investigate how, as new elders, we can continue to heed our calling in the next phase of life. As we move from full participation in the work world to the vocation of elderhood, we can use our gifts in new ways, through mentoring and other sorts of relationships that connect us to others through meaningful work.

Chapter 4: *The Flame of Meaning: Reclaiming Our Purpose* offers guidance for the biggest of the big questions, "What Is My Legacy?" It examines the power of purpose within the framework of the recognition that becoming a new elder is ultimately spiritual work. As we move into the second half of our lives, it becomes more and more clear that the time we spend here on Earth is only part of our overall story. Coming to terms with our spirituality and making friends with death as a teacher are some of the topics examined in this chapter as we find ways to keep the fire burning long after our own life's fire has burned low.

In the epilogue, *Keeping the Fire Alive,* we pull together

the principles and stories of the previous chapters and formulate them into a manifesto for new elders in the twenty-first century. We provide a challenge for all persons in the second half of their lives to live on purpose and claim their place at the fire!

What If This Dream Were True?

As we began work on this book, Dave had a dream that could only have been inspired by the discussions and content. He recalls:

The dream began with my death. I was in an airplane and it plummeted to Earth, killing all of us on board

I found myself in the afterlife, where I was given a unique opportunity. I was permitted to return alive to Earth for 24 hours, during which time I would be able to say my goodbyes to loved ones. I felt a great sense of urgency to communicate my feelings for my daughter and wife, especially. In the dream, I returned home where my daughter was doing her usual 6-year-old things—being willful, testing boundaries, exploring life in ways that would typically make me want to steer clear or distract her with the TV or a video. Instead, I felt incredibly honored to be permitted to take part in her world. In the dream, I put my head right next to hers and absorbed the world from her perspective. I wanted nothing more than to just "be there" with her as she was being.

Similarly, in the dream, I was frantic to spend my allotted 24 hours rekindling the passion in my relationship with my wife. I wanted to set aside all the day-to-day negotiations and compromise that go along with making a marriage work and just get back to the essence of what initially drew us together. Again, in the dream, I remember thinking how vital it was that I just experience my wife, Jennifer, as a person, without trying to impose my expectations or wishes upon her. I just wanted to drink as deeply as I could of her in the time I had left.

When I awoke, I was terribly relieved that it was all just a dream and that I wasn't already dead. But all that day, I couldn't help thinking that, in a way, the dream captured what life is or could be all about. What if, I wondered, I tried to keep in mind what a great gift this life is and how critical it is that I use all the time I have to let those I love know that I love them—not for whom I expect them to be, but for whom they are.

As we move into the second half of our lives, suppose we were to wonder if Dave's dream was, in essence, true? It's certainly a possibility explored throughout history in many works from great literature to popular culture. Think of Dante's journey through heaven and hell as he strayed from the right path, midway upon the journey of life in *The Divine Comedy*. Or of George Bailey's chance to see what the world would be like if he'd never been born in *It's a Wonderful Life*.

Getting a second chance in the second half of life is a desire that tugs at us from the deepest levels. Having an opportunity to rewrite the second chapter by drawing upon what we've learned during the first is a dream we all share.

As we approach our fourth decade, we begin to think a lot about who we are and where we're going. We begin listening to the still, small voice gently whispering "what is my truest purpose?" The "second half" begins at that time in most of our lives—usually between the ages of 35 and 55—when we begin to realize we aren't going to live forever. We begin to seriously value our most precious currency, our remaining time. This universal, sometimes unspoken, realization ignites the desire to live on purpose in the second half.

At the same time, pondering this serves to remind us that what we mean by the "second half of life" is something of a moving target. The Centers for Disease Control and Prevention reports that, in 2001, the average life expectancy for men and women in the United States is about 77 years. So, statistically, most of us enter into the second half when we're about 38 and a half. Our 40th birthdays, of course, are more of a watershed point when we're apt to admit that we're finally entering "middle age." But that's changing, too. These days, at the beginning of the twenty-first century, people turning 50 can expect to live another 30 to 32 years on average. That's up more than a decade from the start of the twentieth century. And with advances in health care and medical technology, who knows how long the second half will be for any us?

Ironically, though, even as the years before us promise to stretch longer, the time remaining becomes more precious. While the perspective gained in the first half of life typically leads to a certain sense of calm in the second half, it also tends to bring with it a heightened sense of urgency.

What if, we may begin to ask ourselves, we do have only a short time left to live? What if, as in Dave's dream, we have but a limited time to finish the unfinished business of our lives? In what ways would we act differently? In what ways would our best and truest purpose show itself in ways that it doesn't now? What would we say that we haven't said? What would we do that we haven't done? How would we contribute in ways we've always wanted to but for one reason or another have held back from?

The realization that we may have a span of years ahead that stretches out as long as our entire adult life so far, combined with the understanding that, at any moment, we may be far past the actual midpoint of our lives, gives rise to numerous questions that cannot be avoided if we hope to retain our sense of vitality and purpose. And yet, as varied as these questions are, we believe they can be summed up by the inquiry we intend to pursue in the pages that follow:

As we move into the second half of life, how do we most fully and authentically claim our place at the fire?

Chapter 1

The Flame of Identity

Recalling Our Stories

New Elder
Richard Strozzi Heckler

At an age when most of his contemporaries were wondering what to do with themselves after retirement, Richard Strozzi Heckler embarked on a new and exciting journey uncommon to men at any stage of life.

The words of the Swiss psychoanalyst Carl Jung seemed to have been written just for him: "Wholly unprepared, we embark upon the second half of life . . . we take the step into the afternoon of life; worse still, we take this step with the false assumption that our truths and ideals will serve us as before. But we cannot live the afternoons of life according to the program of life's morning—for what was great in the morning will be little in the evening, and what in the morning was true will at evening have become a lie."

We cannot tell if we have entered the second half of life solely by counting the candles on our birthday cake. We do not really step into the afternoon of life just because we reach a certain age. To know where we are in the process of becoming a new elder, we must learn to look inside.

When Richard Strozzi Heckler looked inside at age 59, he discovered that living in his 60th year was a time of transformation—a time of spiritual awakening. Instead of answers, he was left with questions: "What exactly does it mean to be an elder? How do elders grow? How is the process the same or different for everyone? Who are the new elders?"

Just as predicted by Jung, Richard had noticed a shift within himself. Noon had passed. He had entered a different part of the day, about which he knew very little. But he was aware of crossing a threshold; he was aware that this was a new stage in his journey.

Many older adults pretend that the second half of life is no different than the first. Billions of dollars are spent by millions of people trying to avoid the inevitable changes that attend the advancing years. Jung wrote that such a person "must pay with damages to his soul." Whether we enter the second half of life on purpose with our eyes open, or against our will with our eyes shut, enter we will.

Richard Strozzi Heckler is entering the second half of life with his eyes wide open. He says, "It's an internal thing, definitely! It's clear I am my own obstacle. To be free in the second half means to release those internal mechanisms that hold me. Freedom now feels much more like extension, engagement, striding into an open field."

Richard is the founder and president of the Strozzi Institute, an organization dedicated to exploring the frontiers of somatic (mind-body) learning and living. Combining a Ph.D. in clinical psychology with a 30-year history as a student and teacher of the martial art aikido, Richard still glows when he discusses his love for teaching—particularly the teaching of young people.

"When I'm teaching younger people, I wake up with a warmth and a fire in my chest that gets me going. I wake up and see a wreath of color—I've been given another day to serve. I hold a genuine feeling of possibility, that there's something out there today that will allow me to help them advance their dreams."

Richard, like many of the new elders we interviewed, has a life that represents an exception to the traditional model of aging in our culture. We spoke with him early one morning while he was making breakfast for a 6-year-old child—his son, not his grandson. At an age when most people his age are launching their children into the world, Richard finds himself in a welcoming space with a second family and three young kids. For Richard, finding purpose in the second half of life involved marrying and starting a whole new family.

"Our world is so open," Richard claims. "There are more options than ever before—more lifestyles and work-styles available. I have choices before me at any given moment to put the best part of myself forward."

In addition to his family, Richard feels the fullest expression of himself emerges through his work. "If I sold my business," he admits, "it would be like selling myself."

Reflecting on what qualities he would look for in a wise elder, Richard names his friend and colleague,

George Leonard. At age 80, George is "still future-looking. He sees the horizon. And he's a stand against ageism!"

According to Richard, "wise elders like George are patient—patient in the sense of having the long and panoramic view. Not just that someone takes time, but that their patience comes from a deep and wide perspective on life. Wisdom is the intelligence and generativity that is beyond the self. Over three billion years of evolution is evident in wise elders. They know how to tap into that and show others how they can tap into it."

Adult life increasingly develops to different rhythms. Some people begin new careers when others their age are concluding their final ones. Some start families at a time others are facing the "empty nest." In this era of choices, new twists and turns are the normal ingredients of growing older. We are free to experiment with new ways to live and work in the second half of life. Some are training for triathalons at 65, while others are headed for rocking chairs. Who would have thought, for instance, that a 77-year-old former astronaut named John Glenn would take another journey into outer space?

The passage that Richard is exploring in his 60th year is not merely a shift from one chronological age to another. As Joseph Campbell put it so well: "The call rings up the curtain, always on a mystery of transformation. The familiar life horizon has been outgrown; the old concepts, ideals and emotional patterns no longer fit; the time for passing the threshold is at hand." Richard Strozzi Heckler is showing us the way across that threshold into a deeper dimension of ourselves.

To age successfully, we must do more than keep fit and stay healthy physically. Like Richard Strozzi Heckler, and George Leonard, we need to stay mentally and emotionally healthy as well by initiating growth to a new level. To do that, we need to deconstruct and reconstruct our stories— we need to pursue self-understanding by poring over the pages of life we have written and making sense of them in context of the chapters now unfolding. Too many people live their lives as a short story that warrants no revision. They live fully for only a short time and extend the dying process far too long. New elders point to an alternative. They show us how the second half of the story can be as vital and compelling as the first.

Rewriting the Story for Our Second Half

To set a path for the second half of our lives, we have to know where we've come from in the first half. "Life can only be understood backwards," wrote Danish philosopher Søren Kierkegaard, "but it must be lived forwards."

At any stage of life, we can review where we've come from and take stock of our lives. But mid-life is a time when it may be possible to recover the life we have lost in living. The inward journey involves the return to our place of origin. Or, to paraphrase T. S. Eliot in "Little Giddings," the end of our explorations "will be to arrive where we started and know the place for the first time."

The process of recalling our stories is one of the critical

steps toward vital aging. It is never too late to begin to know oneself for the first time. The extent of our earlier inability or refusal to honor our stories will determine how long it will take to recover the life lost in living.

Most of us have been too busy writing the story of our life in the first half to be able to read it, Attention to our own stories is partly forced on us by the circumstances in the second half of life. Our children mature and move out, our colleagues retire and move on, our parents and friends grow old and pass away—all of these events focus our minds on who we are, how we've gotten here, and where we're going.

However successfully we've managed to deny death, changes in our bodies make an awareness of it impossible to ignore. Indicators as commonplace as graying hair and slower recovery from injury expose a new—or at least long-neglected—understanding of what it means to live and to die.

With this understanding comes an opportunity to draw and communicate great wisdom from the life we have led, through the recollection and retelling of our life's stories. Of course, many people are reluctant to share those stories. Usually, this is because they feel there isn't much to tell or because they fear revealing secrets. Yet, it is commonplace that from the most ordinary lives often come some of the most extraordinary tales.

Recalling our stories moves us forward and frees us from the wounds of the past by helping us to put our lives in context. Taking stock of the first half of life is a step toward being freer to live the second half with greater vitality. The events of the first half forced us to pay attention to the "doing" of them; we spent more time making things than making sense of them. But there is something about systematically recalling our stories that accelerates the growth process and puts us in a more solid position to move forward creatively.

As we tell our own stories, a new relationship with the world emerges. We move from an emphasis on external matters to a focus on inward feelings, replacing a feeling of outward obligation with a renewed sense of personal purpose. The inward look transforms the outward journey.

Paradoxically, by becoming better acquainted with our own story, we more fully understand the stories of others. We are freed from the perspective of seeing all reality as revolving around ourselves. We continue to be important, but what's around us—individuals, society, all of nature—takes on new significance. We often move from an egocentric view of reality to one that is more universal.

Increased attention to one's own story carries with it a deeper appreciation for the stories of others. Recalling and affirming our own story frees us from the wounds and despair so evident in many older people. Recalling our own story uncovers feelings of kinship with people with whom we have shared times and places. Doing so enables us to rediscover and respect a new and potentially more purposeful way of relating to the world—both within and around us.

Nobody is beyond growth. No person ever reaches a stage where further development is either inappropriate or unwarranted. We all need—and whether we know it or not, want—to keep growing. Of course, there are times when staying on a plateau is legitimate and times when, for good reasons, we hold back from advancing, but overall, there is no denying the truth: We either continue to grow or we begin to die. Recalling our stories is an antidote to such stagnation and a catalyst to growth.

Finishing Our Lives

For many people today, retirement is a roleless role. This is true in large part because the traditional notion of retirement fits with a worn-out notion of aging that conceives of it primarily in terms of disengagement and decline. Today, though, many of us are asking "How appropriate is retirement for a vital person with 30 or more years left to live?" Retirement, as it has been conceived for the past 100 years or so, can turn purposeful lives into casualties.

The traditional story of retirement will no longer be relevant to a growing number of people in the second half of life. It is time to retire that conception of retirement.

James Hillman, in his book, *The Force of Character,* talks about the "finish" of our lives in a way that distinguishes "finish" from "end." Finishing our lives, says Hillman, is better understood as "putting a finish" on our lives—that is, burnishing our character to a high gloss. Hillman makes the natural connections between finishing our lives and distinguishing the legacy we leave. Both require us to develop the most authentic expression of who we are to claim our place at the fire.

Recalling our story is essential to the challenge and privilege of finishing well in life. The true expression of our life's purpose is as vital to our ending as to our beginning. Heeding our call keeps us journeying on purpose—and thus growing and evolving to the very end of our lives. We may retire from our jobs, but there is no relaxing from our individual callings. Calling not only precedes career but outlasts it as well. Callings never end when careers do. We may at times be unemployed or retired, but no one ever becomes uncalled. Our vocational story unfolds from cradle to grave.

Betty Friedan, in her book *The Fountain of Age,* gives a fascinating account of her research into the aging process. One breakthrough insight is that "being old is not the same as acting old." She concludes that the mind plays an essential role, along with the body, in how we age. Our stories determine whether we are growing and heeding our calling or declining and decaying. And according to her research, the almost universally held story for aging is a period of decline. As Friedan observes, "Myth has replaced reality."

We have all seen people who are aging well. Actor-director Clint Eastwood, at age 73, talks fondly about being on the "back nine" of life. Author Jane Juska, in her best-seller *A Round-Heeled Woman: My Late-Life Adventures in Sex and Romance,* tells the story of what happened after she took out an advertisement in the *New York Review of Books* that said: "Before I turn 67—next March—I would like to have a lot of sex with a man I like."

These are obviously not 21-year-olds, but they have the curiosity and hunger for the life experience of a young person. These are people who heed their callings from cradle to grave. These are people who refuse to see themselves as "senior citizens." These are new elders like Vivian Marsh.

New Elder
Vivian Marsh

Vivian Marsh's transition to a more purposeful second half of life happened almost by accident. "And that in itself represents a pretty huge transition," she tells us, "for most of my life I've not been someone who does things unless they're very clearly planned out. My friend Charlotte tells me that this is because I'm a double Virgo—I don't know about that—but I do know that my entire career was built upon organization and preparation. So, it's a been a great adventure to have this new phase of my life more or less emerge by itself, without my having decided beforehand how it would look."

It makes perfect sense that Vivian should have emphasized organization and preparation in the first half of her life. Pursuing a Ph.D. in electrical engineering and earning tenured professorship at a major research university—the only woman in her department and one of only a handful in her field—doesn't happen without a lot of planning ... at least for Vivian it didn't. "I was always interested in numbers, even when I was little. When I was in high school, I took all the math and science classes I could—I was often the only girl in those classes—and I decided pretty early on that I was more interested in the 'applied' side of things than the theoretical. That's how I got into engineering. And I picked mechanical because I've always loved gadgets."

At 53, though, with over 16 years of service in her department, Vivian took her first sabbatical. "That's sort of pathetic, really," she jokes. "Here I am, someone who's supposed to be an expert with numbers, who managed to go more than twice the number of years you're supposed to before taking a break. Sabbaticals are supposed to happen every 7 years; I more than doubled that before realizing it was time."

And during her six months off ("I actually stretched it to nine," she says, "by having the last three months be summer"), Vivian spent a good deal of that time quite literally recollecting not only her own story, but the stories of her family and her ancestors.

"I come from a big Irish-Catholic family and have tons of aunts and uncles, many of whom live within about a ten-mile radius of each other. I've always been the one at family reunions and weddings and such who likes to grill the older folks about the family history. But I'd never done it in any sort of organized way. During my sabbatical, though, I started doing more systematic interviews and writing them up. I also got really into Internet research on genealogy. And one thing I discovered was that there were lots of Marshes out there doing similar research. So, I taught myself some web design and created an interactive website for the sharing of stories and the trading of information. It's been fascinating to hook up with people from around the world who are exploring their roots in the same manner I am—some of whom I'm most certainly related to!"

When Vivian's sabbatical ended, she decided to go back to her department on a half-time basis. "I've sort of done it unofficially," she says, "there had always been a semester here or there in which I taught fewer classes than full-time status, but I had always made up for that time by doing service work. Now, I'm just teaching less without so much advising, committee work, and so on. It gives me a lot more time to pursue a number of other things I'd always been interested in, including, believe it or not, pottery." Here she laughs, admitting it sounds "corny" for a 53-year-old woman. "It's the glazing process I find particularly fascinating. As a scientist, I'm quite intrigued by the chemical changes that take place with the various glazes and different temperatures. As a matter of fact, I'm thinking of writing a paper about glazing for presentation at a conference. Wouldn't that make the 'old boys' squirm in their seats."

The person who is merely aging is a 53-year-old who tries to look like a 21-year-old. The person who is a new elder like Vivian Marsh doesn't mind looking fifty-three, but can engage comfortably with a twenty-one-year-old.

The new elders, like Vivian, neither mourn the passage of time nor deny it. Instead they have chosen a brand new way of looking at their age: Accept the biology but reject the psychology. They accept how old they are, but refuse to let it shape their lives. They have shifted, as Rabbi Zalman Schachter-Shalomi writes, from an "age-ing to sage-ing" outlook on life.

New elders like Vivian Marsh and Richard Strozzi Heckler know they are not just here by chance. They feel connected to those who came before them and in that sense are keepers of their legacies: "wisdom-keepers."

Deep in our souls, we all want to live in a story larger than ourselves. For each of us, the real story is personal and purposeful: to know what we are here to do and why. Søren Kierkegaard wrote in his journal: "The thing is to understand myself, to see what God really wants me to do; the thing is to find a truth which is true for me, to find the idea for which I can live and die."

Since the dawn of history, humans have been pondering

this existential mystery of life. The same question has riddled us throughout our evolutionary history: "Who am I?"

Walking the Talk

One activity that can be of great help in the process of renewing our stories is walking. Sage adults have long sung the praises of walking as a means of self-understanding. "It is a great art to saunter," wrote Henry David Thoreau. Walking is obviously one of the most natural of all human activities and as such, it connects us in a deep way to the natural rhythms of humanity.

This isn't to say that walking is the only way to make such connections; obviously, there are many ways to reconnect to the world around us and recall our stories. Still, many people find the activity of walking and talking to be more natural than sitting and writing. Indeed, there is a great tradition of this: The ancient Greek philosopher Aristotle, for example, made it a habit of doing his philosophizing while walking. Our word *peripatetic* comes from *peripatos,* the covered garden where Aristotle and his followers strolled while discussing philosophy.

Richard recalls contemplating the age-old existential questions while hiking, miles from any town, on the edge of the Serengeti Plain. But he's not exactly alone. A large community of wildebeest surrounds him, poised as if ready for conversation, looking directly at him. These are quiet, unassuming friends, whom he's known for years and he's ready to do some catching up with his bearded companions. In fact, that's why he's there. Africa is a sanctuary when he needs solitude, when he wants to recall his own story.

Richard recalls:

I walk in silence. I recall poet Emily Dickinson describing herself as having an "appetite for silence." In my case, I would say that the appetite is large. To me, incessant societal noise is a disease that can be cured only by going back to the rhythm of silence. These vast, windy hills and plains are a good place to go back to the rhythm. The nothingness fills me. Looking across the Serengeti, I can feel the rhythm. I can feel the Earth inhale and exhale with every breath of mine. The air is heavy with silence, my medicine.

The air is moist and cool. Hiking in the early morning is the best strategy to avoid the intense midday sun and heat. My other friends, the impala, share hillsides with umbrella acacia trees, a classic African scene. Wildlife flourishes around me, both in diversity of species and size of populations. Guinea fowl explode from beneath almost every thorny bush. Thomson's gazelles and zebras are too numerous to count. Hyenas yup and yodel from dusk until dawn. Here, some predatory voice is always calling.

Hiking between the Serengeti and the great Rift Valley, I can imagine hunter-gatherers exploring the same route, foraging seasonally among food resources on the vast savanna. The path ahead is unclear. There are no trails, only animal paths. This is good, since real trails attract people. Not only in location but in attitude, this place is a world away from most places on Earth. Here, evolutionary history floods the senses. One feels the heartbeat of a thousand generations. It's natural to ponder the thought that we all live on the same blue marble that circles the same orbit and subjects each of us to the same gravitational pulls.

The freedom of being off trail sharpens my evolutionary senses and makes me alert. It allows me to discern the sense and essence of my story. It reawakens the instincts that were, at one time, critical to our survival. In the hunter-gatherer world, inattention to small movements and sounds could get you eaten. In the natural world, the story of the universe speaks clearly.

I ponder the recent discovery of skull bones of the earliest known ancestor of humankind in the desert of Northern Chad—a fossil nearly seven million years old that will revolutionize our understanding of our beginnings. The discovery—a nearly complete skull, two lower jaw fragments, and three teeth—is three million years older than any other hominid skull discovered to date. The fossils suggest an evolutionary complexity and diversity in human origins that seem to defy description by the family trees of the past. It plays havoc with the current model of human origins where I'm hiking and because the fossils were found so far from here, long considered the cradle of humanity, scientists conclude that these first primitive hominids ranged much more widely than researchers had expected. It is a stunning find.

As I try to wrap my thoughts around this discovery, I realize that everything in life is natural and an evolutionary part of the story. While I may view life's challenges as an abnormality, an unnatural state, hunter-gatherers hold life's challenges differently. The hunter-gatherer story might suggest that it is normal to have challenges; suffering and death are part of life. This acceptance does not imply powerlessness or disinterest in a meaningful life. What is implicit is the belief that one can enjoy life in spite of adversity. In fact, it is precisely because of our challenges that we can evolve. It is through our challenges that we become more.

I hear a small, still voice within myself. Although I'm walking on terra firma, I feel a shifting of the underlying tectonic plates. It tugs at my story—my beliefs about the origin, nature, and destiny of humankind. This voice speaks to me through centuries of human existence. This voice has been with us since we all were hunter-gatherers, a universal ageless voice. This sense has allowed us, as humans, to survive as a species. I'm convinced that we survived because we recalled our stories here on Earth.

Addressing the Eternities

Human beings survived because some time ago we chose to live a life that addressed not the times but the eternities, as Thoreau put it. Story is what makes us human, after all. Among the animals we, perhaps alone, retain this sense of legacy—this sense that living well means more than just surviving. Lions and birds care for their young, but human beings give to their children something with much deeper nourishment: the notion of story—passing something on to others after we pass on.

As early hunter-gatherers, we might have thought of story in terms of passing along a prized bow and arrows. Then, as time passed and we became more removed from the bush, we might have begun to think in terms of passing along more than survival goods. We likely began to develop a sense that our stories, our experiences, our wisdom were worth passing on to those who survived. We began to pass on something of ourselves—something of the spirit—of who we are and what we have learned.

Hunter-gatherers help us recall the larger story. They are a mirror in which we meet life face-to-face and see our place in it. They whisper our ancient stories to us. They remind us that our purpose has long been to enrich other people's lives through the power of sharing.

An African elder once told Richard that the problem with visiting Africa is that you feel forever in exile after you have left. It's true. That's why he returns year after year. He says, "Many people tell me that they have always wanted to go to Africa, but they cannot explain why. They discover when they do go that Africa reveals to them the ancient human story. It is evolutionary bedrock in some deeper sense. It has a primal draw that truly may be genetically hardwired. I felt that way from my first trek in Africa and I leave with the same feeling today. The trek may be over but my journey isn't."

As descendents of those who started out in the bush, we humans retain this sense of story—this sense that our lives have meaning and purpose, and that living life fully means more than merely surviving. We retain a notion in our souls that goes beyond the natural laws of "eat, avoid being eaten, and procreate."

As time has passed and we have become more removed from the bush and savanna, we have come to understand that there are more ways to nurture the ones we love than by teaching them to hunt and gather. We began to develop a sense of life's lessons that we had learned, and these formed a story every bit as worthy of passing on as the bow and arrows.

So in a very real sense the stories told by elders around the fire, like the Honey Guide story, were the first legacies—lessons to pass on to those who survived. They're stories—as are all our lives—that involve a journey, a quest for truth, a triumph of purpose, and a homecoming. There's a reason that the fireside story has lived for thousands of years. It's essential. And we must continue to claim our place at the fire and tell our stories from generation to generation.

Yet this tradition of the fireside story—or oral legacy— has lapsed over time as we have moved farther and farther away from the natural world. Many people have come to see their legacy almost exclusively in terms of material things. Many people Richard coaches every day increasingly question whether the material world has taken over their lives to the detriment of other, spirited things. His work often uncovers a yearning in people, a desire to pass on more than the material wealth they have accumulated. They want to pass on something of themselves—their story—of who they are and what they have meant. Through our stories we share what is most precious to us—not only what we have earned, but also what we have learned.

From over three decades of working with men and women in the second half of life, Richard has observed that mid-lifers look for some kind of story renaissance—some new vision to guide them and connect them to a new sense of purpose in the second half. The experience of working with these people offers simple proof that in large part we are spiritual beings. Stuff, no matter how much of it we accumulate, is not the way successful people keep score. In the end, it takes a distant second place to a purposeful life.

"Maybe it was synchronicity that led David and me to explore these ideas in a book, or pieces of a puzzle that came together at the same time," Richard recalls. "At around the same time, my wife, Sally, gave me an important book, *Wisdom of the Elders,* edited by David Suzuki and Peter Knudtson. Writing from across indigenous cultures, the elders in the book share expressions of stories to transfer to the next generation. It was a book that drew the distinctions between true wisdom earned through nature and life's lessons and new age wisdom coined for the sake of earning a living. The book struck a deep chord in me. Maybe it was my own aging or the birth of my first grandchild, Austin, that led me to embrace the idea that I would dedicate the next phase of my life to becoming a new elder. I slowly learned that a new view on aging and eldership was evolving within me. The elder within me was coming to the surface and beckoning me to claim my own place at the fire."

Stories With a Purpose

There is a danger in this emphasis on recalling one's story and the potential shift in attitude toward the world that it may imply. We may interpret this focus on recalling our own story as ego-driven, even arrogant. But that assessment arises from a misunderstanding of humanity's inherently heroic nature.

Each of us is born into a particular family at a particular time and place. These historical circumstances are as important as our genetic makeup. Unique advantages or disadvantages, challenges or privileges, opportunities or handicaps are inescapable ingredients of our own story. Neither are we born into, nor do we live our lives, in a vacuum. The combined consequences of the period and place into which we are born define us as surely as does our DNA.

And so, it becomes clear that from the beginning, we are not self-made. Others have provided for our well-being (or not) in a host of ways. And it is not just our parents or guardians who have done so. Unknown strangers who planted trees whose shade we enjoy, forgotten architects of the buildings we work or learn in, anonymous inventors of gadgets that make our lives easier—all these and more are the characters between the lines of our own story. And so, in recalling our story, we inevitably recall the stories of others.

Also, in the process of recalling our stories, we may realize how far our lives extend both into the future and back to the past. The human story carries on. In recalling our own story, we may be inspired about opportunities to act with reference to the legacy we shall leave. Awareness of the future that the young and unborn will inherit is part of our changed attitude toward the external world.

Soon after Dave's daughter, Amelia, was born in 1997, his dad pointed out to him something pretty remarkable. "I know your daughter," he said, "and she's likely to live 80 or so years into the future, let's say 2080 just to round it off. I also know my grandfather, who was born in 1870. That means I have personally connected with the lives of people spanning over 200 years. You know, it's often said that our children and grandchildren make us aware of our mortality; for me, it's the opposite: I'm made aware of my immortality."

Dave's dad's observation is profound: Our lives have great reach, both forward and back. While few of us will live more than 100 years, nearly all of us will have had a direct influence on people's lives over more than two centuries.

What this should remind us of is how much difference our lives do make—no matter what. The mere fact that the range of our influence is so broad ensures that our time spent here on Earth has not been for naught.

Of course, this bestows upon us a heavy responsibility to do something with our time, to make the most of it that we can. But more to the point, it bestows upon us a real sense that we do matter, that we're here for some reason, and that emphasizes, as Dave's dad put it, our immortality.

And when we can tap into this, it can, if we hold it in the proper perspective, give us great hope not just for the future, but for the past, as well. The people we call new elders embody this by living more creatively than ever. Unlike mid-lifers who desperately try to hang on to fading youth, new elders are taking more risks to inspire new growth. They use their profound awareness of the waning number of years they have left to live as an inspiration for how they live their lives.

The ways in which we respond to this potential growth in the second half of our lives will be as varied as our own individuality. To express their purpose, some will plant trees, others will become environmentally active for the first time, others will seek to mentor the young, through writing, speaking, or direct action. The form of the purpose matters little; the desire to benefit future generations is crucial.

Our experience as new elders will be vital to the extent that, by enabling us to reconnect with our own past, it brings about a new relationship to the future. Capable of appreciating the power of the moment, we also care passionately that generations to come will enjoy opportunities as rich as those we have enjoyed.

New Elderstories

Probably all of us have had the experience of being "trapped" with an older person who just goes on and on about his or her life. You're on the airplane, trying to get some work done, and Uncle Joe just won't shut up about his aches and pains and operations. Or you're in the waiting room at the dentist and

Aunt Mary keeps showing you pictures of and talking about her grandchildren.

So, when we think of recalling our stories, this image may come to mind. Having been the "victim" of such storytelling, we may recoil from the very idea of doing so.

But the storytelling we're interested in here isn't just the personal recalling of one's own experiences—although certainly that does figure into it. When we're talking about storytelling here, we're talking about something much broader.

First, it's important to note that the purpose of the sort of stories we're interested in here—we'll call them new elderstories—is different. The primary purpose of new elderstories is not to give the teller an opportunity to simply bend someone's ear or vent; rather, it is to provide some guidance or inspiration first to oneself and, secondarily, to the one being told.

Second, new elderstories have a context that connects them to something more than just the individual. In the telling of new elderstories, we aren't just going on about our own lives, we're offering a perspective that connects our own experience to something more universal.

In the telling of new elderstories, three stories emerge. Each of us begins by articulating "my story"—our own hero's journey, if you will. We move, then, to communicating "our story"—the myths and legends of our own people. Finally, elders learn to articulate "the story"—the common themes of humanity that bind us all together, in all ages and at all times.

The stories of Mitch Albom's former professor, Morrie, in *Tuesdays with Morrie* are a powerful example of such stories. Subtitled *An Old Man, a Young Man, and Life's Greatest Lesson*, the book's central message can be summed in Morrie's statement: "When you learn how to die, you learn how to live." While Morrie talks to Mitch about events in his own life, the stories have a power that resonates beyond the details he provides. Moving beyond Morrie's experience, the stories encompass the emotional realities of Mitch's life, too. Then, expanding even further, Morrie's story comes to articulate universal stories of life and death, as well.

One way to begin crafting such stories from your own life experience is to approach them backward. That is, rather than starting with the personal, start with the universal and think about the experiences you have had that reflect those larger concerns. As a way to approach this, you might start with some of the "big questions" and work your way back to your own story.

This is pretty much the approach favored by the Great American Think-Off, a nationwide competition sponsored by the New York Mills Regional Cultural Center that encourages philosophical reflection by "regular folks." Each year, they propose a "big question" for people in all walks of life to answer. In 2003, for instance, their question was "Do We Reap What We Sow?"

Dave used his own experiences as an unsuccessful child gardener to argue that we don't, in fact, get back from the universe exactly in proportion to what we give out. Whether or not his answer is correct is somewhat beside the point; what was effective about his essay—at least for the Think-Off judges—was that it drew from the personal to comment on the universal.

When we are able to do this, we go a long way toward making connections with others that are illuminating to all parties involved. Dave learned a lot from his experience in the Think-

Off, probably much more than his audience. Nonetheless, it's clear that he touched them in some way; they did, after all, vote him as tied-for-third Greatest Thinker in America!

The Question That Recalls the Story

When we're young, we think that by the time we're old, we'll have it all figured out. And of course, the terms "young" and "old" are all relative.

At age 6, in first grade, we think the 9-year-olds in fourth grade have all the answers. As a freshman in high school, we look at the seniors and are amazed by how together they have it. In our 20s, starting out in our careers, we imagine that by 30 or 35, we'll have everything figured out. What we learn, though, at every stage, is how much more we need to learn.

Most of us were probably taught that by the time we were moving into the "retirement years" that we'd no longer be wondering what life was all about. We'd be old and wise and no longer be questioning what we were doing with our life and why.

But the reality is, the big questions are never fully answered. Living a vital and purposeful life means continually making the very same inquiries of oneself at 60 as one did at 6. We must never stop wondering why we're here, what we should be doing with our lives, who we should be doing it with, and where.

In short, living a vital and engaged life means that we never stop asking ourselves the question, "What Is the Good Life?"

In our book *Repacking Your Bags,* we defined a formula for the Good Life as: *Living in the Place you belong, With the People you love, Doing the Right Work, On Purpose.*

Living the good life means integration, a sense of harmony among the various components of one's life. It means, for example, that the place where you live provides adequate opportunities for you to do the level of work you want to do. That your work gives you time to be with the people you really love. And that your deepest friendships contribute to the sense of community you feel in the place you live and work.

The four elements of the good life—place, people, work, and purpose—continue to beg for attention at every stage of our lives. Just because we are moving into the second half doesn't mean we can ignore the vocation question entirely. (In fact, as we move into a less intense phase, it probably means we need to consider the vocation question more seriously.)

Reflecting upon these elements is a powerful means to recalling your own story. The questions that follow provide you with a framework for thinking about who you are and how you've become that person.

These are essential questions to ask when examining your transition to the second half of life. How you answer them will guide you in claiming your place at the fire as a new elder.

Questions for Recalling Your Story

Question Category: Who Am I?

- What, and how deep, is my spiritual foundation?
- What is my relationship with death?
- Who are my spiritual teachers?
- How present am I in the moment?

- How much time do I take for solitude, reflection, and prayer?

Question Category: Where Do I Belong?

- How healthy is the place I'm living for me?
- How at home do I feel in my home?
- To what extent do I feel I belong in my community?
- What opportunities do I have where I live to do the things I love to do?
- How well do I manage my life so I mostly do what I care about?

Question Category: What Do I Care About?

- Who comes to me for help?
- What are my gifts?
- How am I using my gifts on the things I care about?
- How fulfilling is my work?
- How is the balance of work and play in my life?

Question Category: What Is My Purpose?

- How clear am I of my purpose?
- How aware am I of my legacy?
- What difference am I making in the world?
- Who have I voluntarily helped in the last month?
- What connections do I have to something greater than myself?

Think about these questions in a manner that really encourages reflection. There is no rush; you don't have to answer all of them right now. In fact, the more time you take with them, the more meaningful your answers. Use these questions as a way to dig deeper into your life's story. Take a long look at where you are and how you've gotten here. How can you harvest the wisdom you've gained in the first half of life to sow it more fully in the second half?

Examine your life. What is good about it? What is missing? How do you relate to where you live? How are your relationships? What is happening with work? How are you expressing your purpose? Are you living your own authentic version of the good life (or someone else's)?

All the experiences in your life have brought you to this point in your life. Nowhere can you find better clues to your future than by revisiting and reintegrating the life you have already lived. In no way will you more effectively write the story of tomorrow than by recalling the story of your past.

Recalling the Story Recalled

The value of recalling our stories is twofold: Doing so enables us to better understand ourselves, and it enables us to more effectively connect with others in the world. So one test for whether our recollections are helping us to grow as new elders is to see whether they are inspiring self-awareness and deepening our relationships. Uncle Joe's tired litany of woes seems unlikely to do either of those; the life lessons communicated by new elders like Richard Strozzi Heckler or George Leonard seem to have both those effects.

Dave recalls a story that he often shares with the Philosophy for Children classes he leads.

I tell this story to illustrate a couple of things—the ethical theory known as Utilitarianism and some problems with it—but most importantly, my own steps and missteps in trying to figure out the right thing to do. It's a pretty simple story, grounded, more or less, in the Utilitarian view of right and wrong: that actions are right insofar as they maximize total happiness. That is, actions are right providing they lead, in the words of one of Utilitarianism's seminal theorists, John Stuart Mill, to the "greatest good for the greatest number."

In any case, the story is this: Some years ago, I had very dear friend, Jimmy, who was dying of AIDS. He was a wonderful man, with amazing joie de vivre and a bittersweet gallows humor about the situation in which he found himself. In the last few months of his life, due to the wasting syndrome associated with AIDS, he could hardly eat. He lived, during this time, mostly on bottled water and Triscuit crackers. But with his attitude on life, he found even this strangely humorous, and as a result, developed this sort of ironic fascination with Triscuits. Whenever he would finish a box of them, he'd stack the box next to his bed, building up what he referred to as "The Great Shrine of Triscuit." He joked that when he died, he wanted to be buried in a casket made of the tasty wheat snacks.

I was living in Santa Fe at the time and was planning one last visit to Los Angeles to see him before he passed away. I was shopping around for a gift and found myself in a cooking goods store. As I walked in, I saw, on a small dorm-sized refrigerator, the perfect gift for Jimmy. There, stuck to the door of the mini-fridge were four magnets—Triscuit magnets! Made out of plastic, like the demonstration food in the windows of sushi restaurants, they were perfect replicas of the small square crackers that Jimmy so adored.

I took one off the refrigerator and brought it to the checkout counter. "I'd like to buy this magnet," I said to the shop owner who stood behind the cash register.

"Sorry," she replied. "Not for sale."

I didn't quite get it at first. "No, I'd like to buy this," I said. "Pay cash money for it."

"I understand," she said. "But that magnet isn't for sale."

"Oh, please," I said. "Let me explain." I told her all about my dying friend and his love for Triscuits and how this would be the perfect gift.

"Yes," she said, "I see. But I'm sorry, I had to go all the way to Japan to get those magnets and they are not for sale."

"I'll give you 50 bucks," I said.

"Sorry, not for sale," she replied with finality. "We have many other lovely gift items, and I'm sure if you shop around you can find something. But those magnets are not for sale."

At this point (I tell my audience), I had a decision to make. What was the right thing to do? According to Utilitarianism, the act that maximizes total overall happiness is what's right. So, I had to do a little Utilitarian calculus. I added up how happy Jimmy would be to get the magnet, how happy I'd be to give it to him while keeping in mind how unhappy the store owner would be to have one of the magnets go missing . . . and the answer was clear.

The right thing to do was to steal the magnet.

So, I tucked it into my pocket, browsed around a bit to allay suspicion, and darted out the door. And of course, I was right: Jimmy was delighted to get the magnet—and even more delighted that I had stolen it for him—and I like to think that when he died a few months later, that perhaps someone took it off the metal lamp next to his bed and placed it gently in his coffin.

But now, when I look back at this, it seems to me that I didn't do the right thing—or at least, that I could have done much better. I didn't have to steal the magnet, after all. When I tell this story to kids, they ask me things like: "Did you leave the 50 bucks?" "Why didn't you just make your own magnet using a real Triscuit, some varnish, and glue gun?" One fifth-grade girl said to me: "How do you know that those four magnets weren't given to her by her four children who died tragically, and those are the only mementos she has of them?"

So when I recall this story and tell it, I am not simply—I hope—recounting an event in my own life. I'm also hoping to make a larger point about learning from one's mistakes and perhaps even a larger point about the human experience of trying to do our best but failing.

Students tend to really enjoy it when I tell them this story. It humanizes me, shows how fallible I am, and gives them some insight, I think, into their own attempts to do the best that they can.

Also, each time I recall it and retell it I find I learn something more about myself. I used to tell it simply as an explanation of Utilitarianism. Later, I came to see it as illustrating how difficult it is to determine the right thing to do. Lately, I find the central lesson to be, as I said above, something about human fallibility. And I think as I continue to recall and retell it, I'll discover something else as times goes on.

The point we want to make here is that recalling our stories is not something we do once and then are done with. It's an ongoing process of recollection and revision, one that can help us more fully understand ourselves and help others understand us better, as well. We urge you, therefore, to take advantage of opportunities to recall your own stories and as a result, find new connections to ancient and powerful stories of which we are all a part.

The Fireside Chat

Each of the core chapters in this book ends with what we are calling a *Fireside Chat.* We offer these sections as a way to help you stimulate dialogue with friends, family, and colleagues to keep alive the fire started in each chapter.

We encourage you to literally have a chat around a fire. As we have noted, there is something quite powerful about fire as a stimulant to reflection. Sitting in the dark, gazing at the dancing flames, does something to us as human beings. The fire seems to naturally draw the words from us. Perhaps it has something to do with the calming effect of watching the flames—which were certainly humanity's first "home entertainment center." Perhaps it has something to do with the way fire connects us so powerfully to our human origins. Whatever the case, if you can manage to center your fireside chats around a fire, so much the better.

Even if you can't, we encourage you to make time for these discussions at a time and in a place that encourages thoughtful reflection. Turn off the TV and cellphones. Lower the music. Center yourself by finding your breath. You may want to extinguish artificial lights. We've found it very effective to use candles if a real fire is impractical.

When you and your fireside partner (or partners) are ready, begin your fireside chat.

This fireside chat encourages you do develop dialogue around the recalling of your own life story. It will be enhanced if you conduct the discussion with a person or persons with whom you are particularly close. Dialogue with a close friend, a loved one, a family member, someone who makes you feel good about who you are and who cares for you deeply.

The Firestarter Question

Allow yourself a journey back into and over your life. Consider the many points in your life when you might have made different choices leading to different paths, but at which you made a choice that led to the path on which you currently find yourself. We call these points the "trigger points" in your life.

Imagine a graph of your life. Starting with your birth story, rank the high and low trigger points in your life. Think of the high points as those points at which you made choices whose outcomes you are especially satisfied with. The low points will be those at which you made choices you feel more ambivalent about.

Then, draw a timeline connecting all the points. Reflect on this timeline and consider what it says about the life you have lived—and the life you haven't.

Have a fireside chat centered around the following questions:

- What events do the dots on your lifeline represent?
- Which events made a major difference in the life you have led?
- What are the lessons you take from the choices made at each of the points?

Encourage your fireside partners to all contribute to your story. Help them create theirs. Speak your minds. Speak from the heart. Keep the fire of dialogue alive!

Tending the Fire

At the conclusion of each chapter, we offer this section called *Tending the Fire*. Here you will find additional ideas and/or practices that may help address the question broached in the preceding pages. Consider this section another way to spur dialogue—both with others and yourself—on each flame of vital aging. It's not so much a "how to" segment as a "what if?" or "why not?" piece. You may find it useful to engage in each *tending the fire* activity as you move through the book or you may prefer to set them aside and do them as time permits. Either way, whatever works best to tend your own fire within.

The Flame of Identity: Who Am I?

Most of us will find it difficult to live on purpose in the second half of life unless we contemplate the big picture—unless we recall the first half and reflect upon who we were and how that affects who we are in this new phase of life. Unfortunately, such reflection takes time, something many of us have little of. Reflection, it seems, is becoming a lost art in a world driven faster and faster by new technology and globalization.

But we can't really live purposefully until we know

ourselves. And this means we must—at least occasionally— find some way to hit the pause button, to still ourselves and contemplate the big picture, the overall scheme of things.

One way to do that in context of the flame of identity is to look at your life from the far end of it. Imagine, for instance, you are looking back over your life on the occasion of your 90th birthday.

You have chosen to celebrate your 90th birthday by gathering around a fire with your dearest friends, family members, and colleagues. If you could throw a log on the fire for each time you made a significant difference in the lives of those assembled, would you have a bonfire or a flicker?

The people gathered have requested that you share a few significant stories from your life. Which ones will you choose? What makes those stories special to you?

Think over the events, experiences, and happenings of your life in terms of throwing logs onto your 90th birthday fire. As you do so, reflect on how the following have helped fuel your fire:

- Music, literature, and art
- Spirituality and religion
- Education and lifelong learning
- Vocation and work
- Play and recreation
- Friends and colleagues
- Family and spouse/life partner
- Your own parents and their aspirations for you

What will you do with the second half of your life so that your birthday at age 90 will be celebrated with a roaring fire?

Chapter 2

The Flame of Community

Refinding Our Place

New Elder
Ruth Shapiro

When Dave's dad died, his mom, Ruth, who had lived in the same house in Pittsburgh for over 30 years, decided it was time to move. This isn't an uncommon reaction; major life changes like the death of a spouse often impel us to make changes in our living situation. What was somewhat unusual about Ruth's decision was that she didn't consider heading off to Florida or Arizona or any of the other "elder ghettos" as she calls them. Instead, she thought about what makes a place "home" for her. It certainly wasn't warm weather or an "active elder lifestyle." Rather, what she deemed important was family and independence. Also, having had to take care of her aging mother by long distance, Ruth was determined not to put her own kids into that same situation. When her own mom was in the last years of her life, Ruth was constantly shuttling between Pittsburgh and Cincinnati, where her mother lived. "I just didn't want to put you and your sister through that," she tells Dave. "It was all so unnecessary. The problem is, you know, that people are afraid to admit the obvious—that they're going to die—and so don't make the necessary preparations. For me, the solution was easy; since neither you nor your sister has any intention of returning to your childhood home, then I would come to you. If Mohammed won't come to the mountain and all that."

Ruth spent her first few years as a widow getting the accumulations of 35 years of marriage in order: donating clothes, giving away books, selling the house, and so on. She retired from her long-time job as medical librarian at Braddock Hospital in a suburb of Pittsburgh.

Then, along with the help of Dave's sister, Deb, she purchased a duplex house in Madison, Wisconsin, where Deb was living. It's big enough that they don't get in each other's way, but small enough that they're able to help each other out—Mom assists by being the "responsible adult" to her two teenage grandsons when Deb's away—and Deb can lend a hand as Mom gradually may need more care.

The decision to pack up and leave Pittsburgh, her home of 40 years, was relatively easy for Ruth. That's because, for Ruth, home isn't so much a physical place as it is a matter of one's attitude toward it. "Home is what you do and the people you do it with," she says. "As long as I've got a modicum of culture, some interesting professional activities, and a small group of friends, then it feels like home." Within a month of transplanting to Madison, Ruth had become a subscriber to a theater and a chamber music ensemble, had secured for herself three days a week volunteering at the University's medical library, and was regularly hosting dinner parties for Deb and a growing group of friends and acquaintances.

"I've adjusted pretty well for an old broad of 78," says Ruth. "Madison feels just like home. Of course, it didn't hurt that when I moved, I brought a lot of the old stuff. My living room here looks just like a miniature version of our home in Pittsburgh. And that's comfort. It's what we loved most dearly from our past life. But you can't hold onto all of it; if you do, you lose everything."

The Power of Place

As we move into the second half of life, we inevitably confront the question "Where in the world do I belong?" Changes in relationships, work, and physical health naturally precipitate the need to reconsider our sense of place. And this means both our external place—where we live—as well as a more internal sense—where and to whom we really belong. Fortunately, the second half can provide us with a unique opportunity for renewal; we cannot avoid the freedom to choose whether to stay, grow, or die.

The challenge is to discover the basis on which to choose to move or stay, cling to or renew.

In nature, organisms move about and relocate when the time is right. Migrations are a survival tool for countless numbers of animal species. As contemporary human beings, we seem to have a tendency to hunker down and stay put when we're challenged. But this may not be the most appropriate response. We're genetically programmed for both flight and fight; we need some way to figure out which is the better choice.

In traditional cultures, elders are accorded a special place, both literally and figuratively. The Hadza people reserve a prime spot in the inner circle around the fire for those individuals who have attained the status of tribal elders. They also reserve a special place in their rituals and respect for such individuals.

Contemporary Western culture doesn't do such a good job of holding a place for elders; it's up to each of us, therefore, to claim our place by focusing on that which sustains and renews us. We do this by recognizing what we have to offer to our communities and figuring out the best way to share it. In so doing, we make ourselves a resource for success in our communities and thus carve out the place in which we belong.

Soon after completing the first book he and Richard worked on, Dave and his wife Jennifer, picked up from their home in Minneapolis and headed off to Seattle. They had a variety of reasons for their move, but the primary one was that the Midwest never really felt like home to either of them. They enjoyed Minneapolis a lot, but something about it never quite fit. While they felt, when they were there, that it was a great place to live, neither ever really envisioned settling there forever.

Making the move was complex, difficult, and expensive. It would have been much easier to stay in Minnesota than head all the way across the country with no friends, family, or place to live.

And yet, it was all worth it. In the end, Dave and Jennifer found their home in the Northwest. It's not perfect, and it's certainly wet, but it is the place they belong.

Everyday, people pack up and face the trying challenges of finding a new place to call home. Nobody particularly looks forward to moving, but many of us look forward to having moved. The hunger for a place we belong is among the most deep-seated of our emotions. We're willing to put up with a lot during the journey if the promise of home lies ahead.

The myth many of us have accepted is that as we age and put down roots, we lose our ability to relocate, either literally or figuratively. Often we get stuck in a place, again, both literally and figuratively. Ultimately, though, the only way to get unstuck is to find a better place. The only way to liberate ourselves from the restraints of a place is to claim a new one. Just as no tree can grow tall unless it is firmly rooted in the soil, so we, too, cannot continue to flourish unless we have set down roots in the place we really belong.

Of course, it is a serious challenge to identify where that place is. We can pore over maps all day long, consult the places–rated atlases, and contact chambers of commerce all over the world, but the information we gain won't give us all the answers we seek. Ultimately, the place we are looking for is a place somewhere within us. We must journey inward as well as outward to find our place in the world. Like those intrepid explorers of old who sailed off to *terra incognita,* we too must be willing to venture into uncharted waters. We must be willing to explore the regions of our own world—our internal world—about which the maps provide no information. And to succeed in our quest, we must do more than merely peer over the edge of those maps, we must venture into the unknown as well.

Consulting Our Internal GPS

What sort of tools do we have to find where we belong in the world?

If it were merely a matter of finding a specific place, then the task would be fairly easy.

On any sort of longer trek these days, the global positioning system (GPS) has become invaluable. Such devices, using satellite technology, enable us to pinpoint our exact location anywhere on the planet. But of course, unless we know what we're looking for or where we're going, that doesn't really help us much.

A few years ago, for instance, a friend of ours, Gary, was using his GPS to find the cabin that he and his friends were staying at on a fishing trip in Canada. As they approached the site in their powerboat, Gary had his eyes fixed on the readout of his device. He kept ordering the boat's driver to "go south, go south, go south!" When the driver kept heading straight on, Gary became incensed! "Why don't you go south? It says right here on the device that we need to go south!"

The boat's driver just laughed and directed Gary's attention away from the readout on his device to the shore before them. "Look," he said, "the cabin's right here." And with that, he pulled into the dock and stepped out to their waiting cabin just a few feet away.

The lesson here is that in spite of how effective and useful technologies like GPS might be, we still need to rely on our senses—both internal and external—to tell us where we are.

We need to attune to our innate sense of direction to guide us ... given that we might already be where we're trying to get to.

And this means, as we have mentioned, that we need to think about place as more than just a physical space. All too often, people in the second half of life conceive of place solely in terms of the outward environment. They pack up their belongings and move to a warmer clime, install themselves in a tiny condo thousands of miles from their roots, and then wonder why, in spite of the exterior heat, they feel so cold inside.

A real sense of belonging to a place involves more than just physical comfort. A sense that we are seen by others, that our contributions matter, that we are making a difference and touching people's lives plays an even more vital role in helping us to feel like we're where in the world we belong.

We can assist our internal investigation into where our outward home in the world is by introspection and through discussion with others. Some of the questions we can ask ourselves that will help us in figuring this out include:

- How important to me is climate?
- What sort of physical environment helps me to feel most at home?
- What medical and social services are essential to my sense of safety and place?
- What cultural activities do I need in a place I call home?
- What opportunities are available for me to express my calling through work in this community?
- How important is it to me to be in close proximity to my family?

Answering such questions, preferably in discussion with people you care about and who care about you, can provide an important foundation for truly understanding where we belong in the world and where in the world it is we call home.

New Elder
Betsy Hutchinson

As a woman of "a certain age," Betsy Hutchinson is reluctant to state her true chronological identity. "Women of my generation were taught not to reveal certain things; I suppose I still hold on to that. Let me put it this way," she says, "I'm much younger than my mother was when she was this old."

Betsy is not a young woman, but she exudes a young spirit. Probably that's because she spends so much time around young children. A teacher for a progressive preschool in the Seattle area, her days are filled with negotiating the spaces of 3- and 4-year-olds, kids young enough to be her great-grandchildren. I didn't set out to do this in 'retirement,'" she says. "I taught middle school for 30 years, and when I left the classroom, I was sure I was done with it. My dream was to move to New Mexico and do the Georgia O'Keeffe thing. I was going to wear turquoise bracelets and be a painter."

"Well, I tried it. I sold my house in the Northwest—as a widow, it was fairly easy. I didn't have to worry about anyone else's stuff. And I moved to this great little cottage just outside of Santa Fe. I had my paints, my easel, and I was taking some art classes at the local college. Talk about idyllic. Well I lasted exactly six and a half months. There came a time, about halfway into the thing, where I would get up, get out my paints, and wonder—excuse me—what the hell? I found myself driving by the local elementary school on my way to classes at the college, trying to catch glimpses of the kids playing on the playground. Good thing the cops weren't following me; they might have pulled me over as a suspicious character," she laughs.

"Anyway," she admits, "it became pretty obvious to me that my real home, if you will, is the classroom. Well, with my connections in the Northwest, it was a lot easier to find a way back into one than it would have been in New Mexico. So, I made some calls, set up some interviews, and came back here.

"I always wanted to work with younger children, and I've long been interested in Rudolph Steiner's Waldorf approach to education—something that wasn't really an option as a public school teacher—so here I am. If you'd have told me a couple of years ago that I'd be spending my days these days teaching preschool, I'd have said you were off your rocker. But you'd have had the last laugh, because here I am."

Your Place at the Fire

As we reflect and discuss our sense of place in the second half of life, we want to make sure we don't overlook one of the best and most time-honored ways of identifying where we really belong.

Traditionally, people called a place home for a combination of two main reasons: home was the place they were most needed and the place where their own needs were best met.

When Dave's grandparents, for instance, left their ancestral homes in the Jewish ghettos around Kiev to find a new home in America during the early part of the twentieth century, they did so because their needs to be free to make a living were being prevented by the anti-Semitic Czarist pogroms. But when they settled and stayed in New York City it was because that was where they could best provide for the needs of their children—and then later, their parents, whom they brought over from the old country.

In more traditional societies, these reasons are even more manifest. The Hadza elders, for instance, are accorded their places of honor around the fire because of all they have to offer their people in the way of wisdom and experience. At the same time, they are patently aware that their own survival depends entirely upon the assistance of their fellow tribespeople. Their sense of place is based much more on the relationships they have with their people than with the actual land on which they reside. "Place" is a somewhat fluid concept to hunter-gatherers; since they are so often on the move, the place they are in tends to move with them. And that place is defined by the role that they play within the roving community.

It can be illuminating for us in the contemporary world to tap into this traditional perspective. As you ponder your place in the world, think about where you are most needed. Who depends on you for emotional support?

Now, it's true that one of the common complaints of people as they move into the second half of life is that they are "no longer needed." If this is indeed the case, then it's important that a person find a way to help somewhere. Any number of community organizations are constantly crying for assistance; there's no end of volunteer work to be done. Or, if that's not feasible, then there's always a pet—we're all familiar with the studies that show how older people with pets tend to live longer, healthier lives.

Conversely, we also will learn something about our place in the world by inquiring into where our needs are met. Ram Dass talks about the "wisdom of dependency"—what we can learn from being taken care of. Suffering a serious stroke that left him fully incapacitated for many months, and which subsequently seriously limited his physical abilities, was for Ram Dass, an incredible learning experience. It was a powerful trigger for coming to understand what it means to depend on other people for our basic needs. It was a lesson in mortality that we all must confront sooner or later.

As we age, we will inevitably need help doing some things we used to have no problem with. Ram Dass writes, "Situations in which we become dependent can become transformative experiences for all parties concerned. By allowing ourselves to reveal our need, we allow those around us the opportunity to help, which is a fundamental need we all share."

Ram Dass might also have mentioned that by revealing our needs and becoming aware of the manner in which they are met, we also go a long way toward finding our place in the world. That said, however, it's also important to keep in mind the other aspect of need—that of helping to meet the needs of others—when making that determination.

For instance, the appeal of retirement communities for many people is that they satisfy the need people have to feel safe. The gated communities of Florida and Arizona confer upon their denizens a real sense of being protected. Still, some folks who live there feel spiritually flat; they don't at all feel as if they're living in the place they belong. A good deal of this can be attributed to their feeling disconnected from those they could help out: families, old friends, communities. As Ram Dass reminds us, the urge to help is a fundamental need. And if we're in a place that doesn't need us, where we can't help out, we won't feel we belong.

One of the inevitable effects of aging is that we become less mobile. Our bodies stiffen up, we move more slowly, we become less able (or at least, less willing) to quickly adapt to new places and situations. What we need to realize, therefore, is that if we cannot move so easily physically, we need to find other ways to move, ways that are more inward.

We need to understand that place is not just a physical experience, but an emotional and intellectual one, as well. "Where we are" doesn't refer just to our location on the planet; it also includes the place in our hearts and minds. Finding and changing our place in the world is, especially as we age, as much—if not more—a matter of changing how we think and feel as it is of changing where we live.

New Elder
Keith Kerrigan

At age 56, Keith Kerrigan sold his stake in the high-tech startup he founded. That payday left him relatively free from financial worries for the rest of his life. These days, he partially fills his days by sitting on the boards of a number of nonprofit organizations, including several of his second love, the theater. A good deal of the rest of his time he spends on his first love, the bicycle.

Keith does several week-long to month-long bicycle tours every year. In the most recent year, he did a fully loaded six-week bicycle camping trip across the United States from Seattle, Washington, to Anacortes, Maine, a supported tour of Italy, and three weeks on the British Isles, visiting the towns of his ancestry and a few distilleries.

Keith says, "Being on a bike feels like home; no matter where I am in the world, when I'm on my bicycle, it feels like that's where I belong. And for me, it's not so much a matter of racking up the miles as it is about having a sense of adventure. In the morning, when you start out on a tour, you never quite know what's going to happen. What will the weather be? The scenery? Will there be a killer climb? And most importantly, who will I meet along the way? I used to be in much more of a hurry to get to my destination at the end of the road. Now, if I meet someone interesting, I'm much more apt to just hang out. So what if I only get half as far as I intended; if I've met someone interesting and shared some moments with them, I've gone much farther along in what matters, anyway."

Never the Same Place At All

One more thing we need to keep in mind as we consider our sense of place in the second half of life is that, ultimately, it's a moving target. The ancient Greek philosopher Heraclitus famously said, "You cannot step twice into the same river, for other waters are continually flowing in."

So, even if we stay in the same place, it's no longer the place it was. We're fooling ourselves to think that we can somehow stay where we are for any length of time. Place is a fluid concept; while it's true that "wherever you go, there you are," it's also true that wherever you are is someplace that's new.

Many people have implicitly expected the place aspect of their later years to be the retirement community, a safe, unchanging environment where nothing bad happens. This may be an attractive picture, but it's quite unrealistic. Nothing ever stays quite the same. At every age and stage in our lives, we need to be adaptable. We will always need to be making adjustments so that the place we are is the place we belong.

This means we need to continually introspect about where we are and what makes us feel a sense of belonging or not. We need to ask ourselves the same questions we asked ourselves as young persons trying to find our place in the world. We need to engage in the same sort of exploration by which we found our home earlier in life to rediscover it later in life. And, if like many people, we never really undertook that exploration back then, but rather just let our home find us, we need to do it all over again for the first time.

New Elders
Sam Gould and Janet Tyler

Sam and Janet are card-carrying members of the baby boom generation. They are hardly, at this point in their lives, elders in the sense that our parents understood the word. But they are already making changes in their lives and lifestyles that are helping them to plan for and create a purposeful life in the years to come. For them, the focus is surely on the place issue. A new sense of where they belong has emerged out of events over the past few years.

Both Sam and Janet were born in the early fifties, attended college and participated in various protest movements in the sixties, and worked and succeeded at professional jobs in the seventies, eighties, and early nineties. Sam was a lawyer specializing in contract law; Janet was director of development for a major nonprofit organization. "We both made good money, did good work, and for the most part enjoyed what we did," says Sam. "We also raised two boys and sent them off to college," adds Janet. "And we had lots of fun together as a family; we traveled, skied, typical things, that we enjoyed together."

Both Sam and Janet acknowledge that it seems sort of strange to talk about their lives in retrospect in this way. "Our lives aren't over; we're both just in our 50s. I'm still working with my firm; Janet is still doing consulting; we still see our boys pretty regularly. It's just that over the past few years, we've made some transitions that are setting us up for what comes next for us, whatever that is."

When they were first starting out in their careers, Sam and Janet had a plan to "get back to the land," as they call it. "I guess it was sort of the sixties-influenced dream," says Janet. "You know: we would both take these jobs, and make just enough money to leave them and buy a place in the country where we would raise organic vegetables or whatever. It didn't exactly work out that way."

As young adults, both Sam and Janet found they enjoyed their work; the reality of giving up all their education and training to become farmers wasn't as appealing as the dream. Plus, then the kids came along and life got more complicated. There was the issue of schools to consider and then extracurricular activities, friends, girlfriends, the whole thing. Even if they were still fully committed to their original plan, it wouldn't have been very easy on the family to make it happen.

After their second son went off to college, though, things changed a bit. "Sort of by degrees," says Sam, "Janet and I began to reconsider our original idea. Of course it was different now. Now it was more about feeling a more direct connection with nature than it was about being self-sufficient hippie farmers."

So, over the course of a couple years, Sam and Janet found a small place with a few acres of land in a rural part of Washington about three hours from their home in Seattle. They are gradually transitioning to live there full-time. They've sold their house in Seattle and currently, rent a condo in town where Sam stays for the four days a week he spends at his office. Janet joins him there when she has consulting work in town; otherwise, she is out in the country.

"I still plan to be fairly active in my firm for about another ten years," says Sam. "It's not like I've retired. But I have begun to think a lot more these days about life after work. And having a place where I can have nature all around me is something both Janet and I have always wanted. In a way, whenever I'm out there, and even though it's only been a couple years we've had the place, I really feel like I've come home again."

Neither Sam nor Janet has an entirely clear picture of what the second half of life in their new place will be for them. They joke that maybe they'll try their hands at some winemaking. "That seems like a noble profession for a couple of old codgers," says Janet. Sam jokes that he'd rather have a still.

Moreover, neither is entirely sure that their current plan is one that they will stick to. "It seems right for now," says Janet. "And I think probably because it's something we always wanted to try. If we never gave it a go, we'd have always wondered."

Sam and Janet realize that the place they currently feel they belong may not always be the place. But they also realize that continuing to have dreams and pursue them is key to a vital and meaningful second half of life.

Fireside Chat
Where Do I Belong?

This fireside chat encourages you to develop a dialogue around the issue of your place in the world. It will be enhanced if you conduct the discussion at a place in which you feel particularly at home. An outdoor environment, especially one around a fire, is ideal; however, what's most important is a place that inspires feelings of comfort and safety.

The Firestarter Question

What are the aspects of a place that will make it home for you in the second half of life?

As you sit around the fire (literally or figuratively), really try to develop a sense of being grounded where you are. Imagine that you are in the place that most fully expresses your sense of belonging. Reflect on it. What is it about this place that makes you feel so at home? Or not? Have a deep conversation about where you've come from and where you are in the world. Encourage your fireside partners to contribute to the discussion. Speak your minds. Speak from the heart. Keep the fire of dialogue alive!

Tending the Fire

The Flame of Community: Where Do I Belong?

The proverb "Where there is no vision, the people perish" is true for us as individuals, as well. To live vitally in the second half of life, we must have a vision of what's ahead. Of course, as our past grows longer, it's easier and easier to get caught up in it. And yet it is precisely because our past becomes weightier that our vision for the future must be more uplifting.

"Imagination is everything," wrote Albert Einstein. So when we are contemplating our vision for the second half of life, it makes a huge difference to imagine a world of new elder models. We want to think outside the gray box of traditional elderhood and envision people who are being the sort of new elders we aspire to be.

Who is living the second half of life in the way you most admire or envy? Who is doing the kind of work you most wish you could be doing? Imagine what their day-to-day vocational experience must be like. What do they have in their personal relationships that you wish you could have in yours?

What would you be doing if you were ten times more courageous in the second half of your life than you were in the first? Where would you be living? With whom? At 90 years old, how would you answer the question "What are you most proud of in your life?"

New elders are people who have asked and answered questions like this in their own ways. They give us new models of aging to which we can aspire in the second half of our lives. We can identify in them certain characteristics that we would like for ourselves. Their courage, commitment, and vitality can be an inspiration as we envision our own futures. Consider people who have and who continue to challenge old ideas of what it means to be old. People like astronaut John Glenn returning to space at age 77. Singer Lena Horne still touring at 85. Rolling Stone Mick Jagger still rocking at age 60. Writer Gore Vidal still crafting insightful provocative essays at age 75. Choreographer George Ballanchine still making dance in his 80s. Actor Clint Eastwood writing, directing, and performing at age 73. Philosopher Bertrand Russell protesting on the streets against the Vietnam war in his 90s. Mother Theresa still helping the poorest of the poor in India well into her 80s.

Who are your own new elder role models? What new images of aging inspire you?

Chapter 3

The Flame
of Passion

Renewing Our Calling

New Elder

Mike McGuire

When we get our first job in our late teens or early 20s, we
know very little about ourselves. We may be aware of our
dreams and ambitions; we may have a sense of what we
like best to do and what we do best—our gifts and talents—and we may know something about how to express
those gifts insofar as our schooling has revealed them. But
in terms of vocation—of what we are really called to do
in the world—most of us are basically clueless. We have
very little idea of what we're really here for, of what sort of
work truly fulfills us, of what we're doing with our lives
beyond earning a living, as opposed to making a life.

   Unless we're one of the lucky ones, like architect Mike
McGuire.

   Right after his 50th birthday, Richard and his wife,
Sally, spent about a year restoring a house on a river they

loved, the St. Croix. At times, the restoration was far from restorative—at least to their mental and emotional health. All the detail—windows, floors, the knobs on the cabinets in the kitchen—had to be considered and reconsidered. At times, Richard and Sally felt more like contractors than coaches. And yet—and in no small part thanks to their architect, Mike McGuire, it turned out to be worth it. Thanks to Mike's help, the end result is a place where Sally and Richard feel they belong and where they feel a sense of belonging.

By the time most of us reach the second half of life, we are quite experienced with the world of work. We know what it means to have a job and to fulfill our responsibilities quite capably and even creatively. But by the time we reach the second half, just as many of us feel a stronger-than-ever-before need to express ourselves more fully through our work. It's no longer enough to simply have a job, even a good one, or even a career; we want something that enables us to express what we feel most strongly needs doing in the world and to have that expression touch people's lives. A vital part of vital aging is passion—doing what we care about.

Mike McGuire thrives on the passion he has found his entire professional life as an architect. "I can't remember a time when I wasn't creatively challenged," he says. "Oddly, I never set out to be an architect; I was interested in painting. But architecture was a way to survive in society without having to have a routine life. Even today I get excited about designing a simple two-car garage."

Mike is someone who is responding to a powerful calling within him; he is living his vocation. The word vocation comes from the Latin root *vox* meaning "voice," or *vocare*—"to call." In the second half of life, many people are still seeking work that does more than pays the bills: work that allows them to speak from this voice deep within. Many such people—those who despair at finding their calling—feel abandoned. "Abandonment" literally means "to be uncalled," to be without a clear destiny. This feeling happens even to the most thoughtful, self-aware people.

At age 74, Mike plays tennis with people in their 50s and 60s. "They can't understand why I'm not retired. I can't fathom retiring. My definition of hell is living in some retirement community in Phoenix with people who all look like me! I'm still trying to create buildings that change lives. That's still my passion."

Mike brings a painter's passion to his life and work. In fact, painting has been one of his passions his entire life. "Most of my friends are younger than me," he says, "and I serve as some kind of mentor for many younger artist-types. I always ask them, 'Where would you go, anywhere in the world, to see art that moves you?' And I'm always startled when they come up empty; they can't think of any place! It's amazing to me. When I was a young architect, I drove clear across the country to visit a well-known architect I didn't know but whom I admired. I parked in front of his mailbox and waited for him to show up. He didn't have a clue who I was or what I was doing in front of his house. But within five minutes of sharing my passion with him, he realized I was a brother! That's the passion I look for in young painters today."

Community—a real sense of belonging—comes through shared passions. "I used to think of my place as my town," Mike explains. "Now I'm more concerned with my country. I'm more interested now, than ever, what makes a place 'the place.' Painting is like putting a message in a bottle—I'm trying to express my sense of place in the world."

What Do We Do With the Rest of Our Lives?

Living on purpose in the second half of our lives presents a unique opportunity and a great challenge. It's an opportunity because, for many of us, the second half of life represents the first real chance we've had to define ourselves and to live in a manner of our own choosing. The challenge that comes along with this is that it's up to us to decide what we really want to do with the rest of our life.

And that means it's up to us to figure out what we really care about.

Most of us, for most of our lives, have our days pretty well mapped out in advance. From the time we were little kids, except perhaps for summer vacations, nearly every day has an agenda of some sort. We get up, go to school, take part in our extracurricular activities, come home, eat dinner, study, and go to bed. As adults, it's pretty much the same, just with work replacing school. But suddenly, if we retire, everything changes. Our days stretch out before us, a vast and uncharted territory. Nobody's telling us when to get up, when to go to bed, or what to do in the meantime.

At first, this can be very liberating. Sleeping late, outdoor recreation, gardening, travel—all the things we've been putting off for years, these are the activities we look forward to filling our days with. Soon, however, many people come to the realization that 24 hours is a long time. "I can only play so much golf," is how one older gentleman we know put it.

Human beings are essentially herd animals. We need to be part of something; we need to be needed. Unless we feel useful—somehow, some way—we find it extremely difficult to carry on. Statistics bear this out. An inordinate percentage of older adults die within 24 to 36 months of retirement. People come to feel they have nothing to live for and pretty soon, they don't. It's a self-fulfilling prophecy that prophesies doom.

In the hit movie, *About Schmidt,* Jack Nicholson plays Warren Schmidt, a 66-year-old man who, after retiring from a lifetime in the insurance business and subsequently losing his wife of 42 years, comes to see his life as totally meaningless. Near the end of the movie, he reflects, "I am weak. And I am a failure. There's just no getting around it. Relatively soon, I will die . . . maybe in 20 years, maybe tomorrow. It doesn't matter. Once I am dead, and everyone who knew me dies, it will be as though I never even existed. What difference has my life made to anyone? None that I can think of. None at all."

Tragic sentiments indeed. And yet feelings that are not at all uncommon to many people in the second half, especially as we transition into the post-work phase of our lives. Without the daily structure of the workaday world, we lose our bearings and feel lost. Suddenly finding ourselves with all-too-much time for reflection, we look back on our lives and wonder what was the point. Not surprisingly, many of us, like Schmidt, conclude that there wasn't any point, that our entire existence has made no difference to anyone at all.

It doesn't have to be this way, though. There's no reason we can't live on purpose during the second half of our lives. This gives rise, however to one of the most basic of all questions: Why do I get up in the morning?

New Elder
Sri K. Pattabhi Jois

Not very many 88-year-old men are up at six in the morning to lead a class of some 300 people in a vigorous 90-minute series of yoga poses. Even fewer do so after traveling halfway around the world from their home in India to major cities in the Western hemisphere, including London, New York, Los Angeles, and San Francisco. And even fewer do this in addition to maintaining a year-round schedule of daily teaching at a world-class center that welcomes students from all four corners of the globe. All of which makes Sri K. Pattabhi Jois, the founder of Mysore, India's Ashtanga Research Center, and longtime teacher of Ashtanga Yoga, even more unique and amazing. His work has touched the lives of thousands for well over half a century and continues to do so in profound ways even as the beloved "Guruji" comes closer to his ninth decade on the planet.

How is it that some people, like Pattabhi Jois, maintain a vibrant and vital life well into their latest years whereas other people pretty much give up and die soon after retirement? Health, of course, has something to do with it; Pattabhi Jois, as a result of his many years of intense physical training, is extremely fit for a man of his age. But that's not all: Many healthy people are pretty miserable in their later years, and many people suffering all sorts of physical afflictions retain a positive attitude all their days.

The real key to aliveness in our later years is to touch the lives of others, especially those younger than us. But while the older we get, the more of those younger people there are, it's not always easy to find avenues for connecting. It takes courage, flexibility, and probably a bit of luck. But those who do make the connections usually experience a heightened sense of energy and passion. And that's not so bad for an old guy.

Bridging the Divide

Obviously, one thing that everyone who is entering the second half of life has in common is that we were all, at some point in our lives, in our first half. Ironically, all the time we spent in those years is no guarantee that we'll have any great insight into the experience of them—especially when it comes to imaginatively conceiving of the experience of others. Getting older, in other words, is not necessarily very good preparation for understanding and connecting with the young. Dave knows this well. He was teaching a philosophy class at an alternative high school called Nova. He says:

It was a fairly mortifying experience in many ways, just like my own high school years. But I learned something very important in the process.

This high school didn't require the students to attend classes; they could go or not go to class as long as they completed the required assignments according to a contract they had developed for the class. So, I never knew whether I would have any students when I showed up to teach.

The school had a central meeting area, a kind of lounge where students would congregate and decide whether to head off to class. I would arrive and be obliged to entice the students in my class to leave their friends and come to our classroom. This was the part that felt like my own high school experience: I had to be interesting and funny enough to get the cool kids to talk to me. If I was—and this was often a challenge when we were scheduled to discuss some rather esoteric aspect of the philosophical canon—then I'd be able to pull together a class. If not, then I'd hang around feeling embarrassed until the class period was over, at which point I could go home and lick my wound by writing a required assignment for the college classes I was teaching at the university.

The first three or four times I went to Nova, it was pretty much a disaster. I tried holding forth about the philosophical topic we were scheduled to discuss. A few kids might show some interest, but as soon as I began presenting the "official" view on the subject from philosophical experts like Descartes or Kant or Plato, their interest and attention immediately waned, and I was left sitting on the couch in the lounge, just me and my Classics of Western Philosophy text.

One day, though, after I'd been going to Nova about a month (my class met just once a week), I arrived to find the students in an extremely animated conversation about a protest against the World Trade Organization's upcoming meeting in

Seattle. I was fascinated both by the students' ardor for the subject and their fairly high level of familiarity with the issues. So, instead of trying to lead the students away into a discussion of what I was interested in, I joined into their conversation. Instead of positioning myself as an "outside expert," I came as an equal participant.

In the course of our ensuing conversation, though, I had a number of opportunities to contribute philosophical perspectives that the students weren't at all familiar with. I actually was able to cover a good deal of the material I had intended to explore that day. But it emerged out of the passions and questions of the students, as opposed to the pre-set agenda of what I thought they should be studying.

From that day on, I never came to Nova with a set agenda. I had lesson plans, sure, but I modified them on the spot depending on what the kids wanted to talk about. They came to be pretty interested in the material we were exploring and we managed to cover just about everything on my syllabus, but we did so in a manner that was driven by their interests, not mine.

What I learned from this was that if I wanted to engage these young people, I had to start from where they were. Eventually, they might come to be curious about the material I hoped to explore, but that wouldn't happen by my announcing it. If the philosophy wasn't relevant to them, they would reject it. But if they found that it had some value to their own lives, they ate it up. They sought out my knowledge and were eager to have me help them understand the material more fully. But it had to be on their terms, otherwise the project was doomed to—if not failure—at least my unending embarrassment.

Dave's experience can be a reminder to all of us who, as new elders, seek to engage young people in any sort of enterprise. Too often, we forget that the so-called wisdom we have to offer won't be appreciated as such unless it makes a difference in people's lives. All our experience in the world means little to others if it doesn't relate to what they care about. From the perspective of youth, there are lots of crazy old people who talk to themselves about the past; there are far fewer new elders who engage them in issues relevant to the present.

The challenge, then, is to stay connected to the historical sources of our own wisdom while simultaneously remaining in touch with the current and future concerns facing young people in the world. This can be difficult to do, but the good news is, if we remain attuned to the indicators, we will receive much of the guidance we need to succeed. They're out there, we just have to learn, as do the Hadza with the Honey Guide, how to look.

Lengthening Our Arms

One thing young people generally have little difficulty doing is expressing their needs. This doesn't mean, however, that others—especially those with more history and experience—will understand what is being expressed. The question then becomes: How do we learn to listen? How do we learn to hear what others are saying . . . when they may not even be entirely clear on what they're saying themselves?

Most of us, when we pass through our 40s or so, have some experience with becoming farsighted. There comes a day when the newsprint seems to have gotten smaller; we wonder why they've started printing the baseball box scores so tiny. We try to hold the paper far away enough from our eyes that we can read it; we discover, though, that—in what seems the mostly "likely" explanation—our arms have become too short. If only we could lengthen them, we'd be able to read perfectly; if only we could hold things steady a bit farther away, we'd be able to see fine.

Simple as it is, this may be an appropriate metaphor for how to engage the interests and concerns of those younger than we are. Instead of trying to focus in on the close-up view, it may be more effective to stand back some, to lengthen our focal point as a way to see things more clearly.

Consider again Warren Schmidt. When he tried to move in too closely on his daughter's life, when he attempted to micromanage the details of her wedding and marriage, she roundly rejected him. But when he stepped back, when he turned the spotlight around and allowed another to see him (as he did with his pen-pal Ndugo), he had great success.

Of course, it's tough to feel as if we're making a difference when people, especially young people whom we are trying to connect with, aren't responding to us as we'd most like them to. And it's certainly the case that every generation needs to make its own mistakes.

However, if we rediscover our passions and live in a manner consistent with them, we can't help but engage others, young and old, in the work that gives our life meaning.

Embracing Life

Psychologist Erik Erikson suggested that in mid-life we confront the essential task of caring for future generations. He called the development of this special form of caring "genera-tivity." Much recent research supports this notion that social caring is an essential ingredient of vital aging. George Vaillant reports in his groundbreaking book, *Aging Well,* that people who successfully embrace the task of generativity at mid-life are three times as likely to be happy than those who don't during the years that follow. Many people who report aging successfully also say that they are experiencing a greater sense of purpose, compassion, and generosity than in the first half of their lives.

We see this all the time in the lives of vital elders around us. People who, in the second half of their lives, are contribut-ing something of meaning to others in the first half of theirs, typically impress us with their energy, liveliness, and joy. Nor has popular culture failed to recognize this either.

In the classic 1970s comedy, *Harold and Maude,* Ruth Gor-don plays Maude, a 79-year-old woman whose consummate zest for life ultimately overcomes the world-weary angst of 20-year-old Harold, played by Bud Cort. At the beginning of the film, Harold is obsessed with death; he fakes suicide dozens of times and attends funerals of strangers just to feed his mor-bid curiosity. Life for Harold is nearly devoid of meaning; he has no real passion for anything; he's just going though the motions, waiting around to eventually die himself.

Maude, by contrast, is a life lover. Even though (as we eventually learn) she is suffering from a terminal disease, she embraces everything in and about the world. She loves ani-mals, sunsets, and flowers and drinks in all the beauty and joy she can find.

As the story unfolds, Harold eventually comes to adopt

Maude's attitude. It happens slowly, over time, through a series of adventures in which Maude helps Harold to see how wonderful life really is—at least when you believe that it is.

The source of Maude's zest for life is her love for all of humanity, which she calls "her species." Whereas Harold wants little or nothing to do with anyone, Maude wants everything to do with everyone. She gets off on talking to strangers and delights in conversations with people from all walks of life.

Harold comes to love Maude and her way of looking at the world. As a result of her influence, he, too, learns to embrace life. Even when, at the end of the film, Maude passes away, Harold sees the beauty in the circle of life. In the movie's final scene, he strums a banjo hopefully, Maude's spirit carrying him forward to the future.

In many ways, Maude is a model for what it means to be a new elder and what it takes to live a vital and generative life for all of one's life. She never stops caring about the world and the people in it; she never stops being a learner; and she never stops wanting to make a difference in the lives of others.

Since we are not all 79-year-old women with a wonderfully eccentric view on things, it may be somewhat more challenging for us than it was for Maude to engage the affection and interests of young people. Most of us already have quite full lives that do not (as does Maude's) involve attending random funerals and stealing the cars of attendees. This doesn't mean, however, that we can't find creative and effective ways of caring about future generations in a manner that gives meaning to all parties involved. The structure of our caring creates meaning in our lives.

It's Not What's On the Outside

Few if any of us are completely immune to the attractions of eternal youth. Most of us wouldn't mind appearing younger and having the physical energy we did as teenagers. And sooner or later, nearly everyone tries to turn back the clock one way or another with a new diet, a revamped exercise program, a fresh wardrobe, a dye job, or even a little nip-and-tuck here or there. There's nothing wrong with any of these approaches, as long as we keep in mind that they are working on the form of things, rather than its essence.

Aging has inevitable physical manifestations, and it's perfectly natural, especially in contemporary culture, to want to limit those to some degree. But it's a mistake to think that just by making ourselves look younger, we somehow will be more able to stay young and stay connected.

Dave knows this firsthand.

Some years ago, feeling the first real intimations that I wasn't a youngster anymore, I undertook a pretty complete overhaul from the outside in. I bought some new "vintage" outfits, upgraded my CD collection, got new eyeglass frames, and even dyed my hair blond in hopes of connecting more completely with my younger self as well as my younger colleagues, students, and community members. I wouldn't say it was totally unsuccessful; I loved the amazed reactions of the fifth graders I was working with when I showed up with bleached hair, but a few incidents really brought home to me that it's not what's on the outside that enables us to connect across the years; it's what's on the inside.

The first of these is a simple comment made by one of my fifth grade students, a remarkably self-possessed and insightful girl named Sophie. While most of her classmates were shocked and/or delighted by my surfer-dude coiffure, Sophie just looked at me curiously and asked, "Why did you do that? Maybe you think you *look* younger, but anyone can see it makes you seem so old!"

Of course, she had hit the nail on the head. While my new "do" may have made me appear younger physically, (and that might be debatable, too) it doubtless also—to people with real insight—made me look more like an old guy trying to look young. And nothing makes someone seem older than that.

Second, while appearances can be deceiving, even pleasantly so, they don't really change the reality of the situation. So, when I went out one evening to see a concert by a band popular among kids young enough to be my kids, my bleached blond hair and groovy retro vintage threads didn't change how weird I felt when the band launched into a song advocating the annihilation of baby boomers.

Ultimately, I felt as if I was wasting a lot of my time focusing on the form of things rather than the essence. If I wanted to connect better with young people, instead of trying to look like them or act like them, it made more sense for me to get a clearer idea of what I could offer them.

So, for instance, at that time, I was also teaching a philosophy class to ninth through twelfth grade students at an alternative school-within-a-school program at a large suburban high school. Their interests were quite varied, but they shared a common zeal for challenging the status quo on issues with implications for social and political justice. Many, for instance, were animal rights activists; others held strong views about the enforcement of drug laws; still others had strong convictions about abortion rights. What I was able to offer them, and what they responded quite positively to, was some in-depth analysis of arguments in support of or contrary to their positions. We spent about a month together developing justifications for and against the various views they held. A number of students were quite excited about having better tools to argue for their beliefs. Some students even came to modify their positions as a result of exploring the arguments pro and con.

For the most part, they came to really value the guidance and direction I was able to offer. I felt as if they appreciated me for who I was, not what I looked like; they came to see me as a valuable resource in their ongoing education and development.

Plus, it didn't hurt that I agreed to dye my hair blue if they all completed their assignments on time. They did, and I did, too.

Younger Elders

We have suggested on a number of occasions that becoming a new elder is not solely a matter of chronology. There's no guarantee we will get wiser just by getting older. That said, there is certainly a correlation between age and wisdom. The lessons we explore in this book are primarily for and from people in the second half of their lives.

That said, there is still much we can learn from people who are much younger than we are. As a matter of fact, one of the most enduring qualities of new elders is their willingness to be open to and appreciative of learning from people in the first half of life. Socrates, of course, spent most of his time talking to the youth of Athens—and in fact, was accused of corrupting them. But just as much, it was they who "corrupted" him.

Andrew G. was the oldest kid out of twelve in Dave's summer philosophy class. Most of the students were getting ready to enter sixth grade; Andrew was going into seventh. All the boys in the class were constantly trying to wrestle with him; they all viewed Andrew as the alpha male. All the girls in the class were constantly teasing him and messing with his stuff; they all had crushes on him. Andrew took this all in stride, though. He had a great sense of humor and a very mature outlook on life. He was the classroom peacemaker when things got out of hand. On numerous occasions, he broke up arguments with a joke or kind word. He also was an instigator for fun; he's the one who lobbied Dave to let the class watch Monty Python movies—episodes that had philosophical import, of course.

Andrew emerged as a real classroom leader; he embodied many of the qualities of a new elder: He knew who he was; he knew where he belonged; he cared deeply for things; and he had a sense of his life's purpose. It didn't matter that he was two months shy of his 13th birthday; he was still the wise elder to his classmates in the classroom community.

Jasmin W. was student body president at the University of Washington. A senior, she had been active in campus and community politics throughout her four years in college. She was an activist for social justice, a fighter for affordable tuition, and passionate advocate for underrepresented student groups. Her commitment to the common good characterized her entire tenure as student body president and typified the wisdom she embodied at a mere 21 years old. She too was a younger elder.

Jake M. was making his third trip to Israel as a member of the International Solidarity Movement—ISM a nongovernmental, nonpartisan group of internationals who make regular pilgrimages to the occupied lands in the West Bank and the Gaza Strip to bear witness to the ongoing conflict between Palestinians and Israelis. Jake became involved with the ISM after his two-year tour in the Peace Corps; this followed four years of writing and editing an alternative newspaper called *Ruckus,* a publication of a student-run anarchist collective in Seattle. Jake's decade-long commitment to social justice made him a wise elder among his ISM colleagues. They depended on his vision, his experience, his commitment to solutions that worked for all, and his calm perspective on the often quite dangerous situations in which they found themselves. Jake was only 25 years old.

These three examples highlight an insight that bears repeating: Being a new elder is not entirely a chronological state. While most new elders are indeed somewhat older (especially than these examples), it is important to remember that becoming a new elder is more a state of being than a number on one's driver's license.

For those of us who are of an age more commonly associated with people who are elders, this is an important thing to remember: It's not how old we are, but how whole we are. Being an elder is more about growing whole than growing old.

New Elder
Richard Peterson

The word "elder" itself often produces negative reactions. Many people in their second half assume that "elder" refers to someone older than they are. Fifty-year-olds think elders are at least 60; 60-year-olds think elderhood starts at 70; 70-year-olds push it out towards 80.

When Katherine Hepburn, in the film *On Golden Pond,* tells Henry Fonda that they should get together with another "middle-aged couple" like themselves, Fonda replies, "We're not middle-aged. People don't live to be a hundred and fifty!"

Many of us resist using any word that connotes "elder" to identify ourselves because it drives home two truths: one, that we're not young anymore, and two, that life has an ending point—and it's not 150!

In the process of denying aging, many dismiss the signals, hoping that by ignoring them, they will go away. Not Richard Peterson, however.

Richard's discovery of a major signal of age—prostate cancer—gave him, he says, a clear message: "It's time to wake up! Something was happening to me; I was undergoing a transformation and cancer was the signal. I could choose to deny it, but ultimately, I had to recognize that my passage into elderhood was beginning. I needed to get on purpose with my life.

At 68, Richard has become one of the premier life and financial coaches in the country. Following a successful executive career, including the presidency of both Vail and Durango Ski Corporations, he reinvented himself at the Hudson Institute in Santa Barbara, California.

"For me," he says, "coaching is a creative experience. I have discovered that I can access what I need to help my clients get what they need. I just don't have room for a grumpy day anymore. Through my experience with cancer, I am now able to wake up and be totally grateful. I'm alive for life. My purpose is to show up for every day with a smile."

The cessation of old self-limiting patterns and the initiation of new healing ones are tangible evidence of the transformative power of purpose in the second half of life. These endings represent a kind of death while the new beginnings are a form of rebirth—a means by which we take ownership of our emerging wisdom and claim our place at the fire. When we focus our energies in this way—body, mind, and spirit—we can change deeply ingrained patterns of behavior in the second half of life. Indeed, new elderhood is possible only when it draws from these deeper spiritual dimensions.

"Becoming an elder," Richard claims, "means being with the people I love, in the place I love, doing my coaching work on purpose. I can honestly say that there is not one of my current clients whom I don't love. And I don't have relationships anymore that are toxic. A high percentage of my clients are in their 30s and 40s. They chose me because of my age—they want me as a mentor; they want my 'wisdom.'"

Richard defines wisdom as "being able to access what's really important in the moment. I'm living with cancer. It's there all the time. I want to live in the moment as many days as possible with the highest quality of life that I can. The wisdom is to keep things simple and to push the unessential aside. Cancer keeps me present."

Old Ideas for New Times

In our earlier book, *Whistle While You Work: Heeding Your Life's Calling,* we explored the topic of calling, which we defined as "the inner urge to give your gifts away." Our calling is expressed in the things that we do most naturally, those things we do well but never had to learn. We respond to our calling by bringing forth our gifts on something we care deeply about. Meaningful work, at any stage of life, is work through which we express our calling on projects about which we are passionate.

John Davis discovered his calling rather early in life; finding a way to express it took somewhat longer. Today, although he is a bit younger than most of the other new elders we profile, John nevertheless has the sort of passion for his calling that is typical of new elders. And perhaps more typically, the expression of his calling has had a wide-ranging effect, one that has allowed and inspired others to passionately express their callings as well.

When John graduated from art school, he didn't know what to do with himself or his degree. Ultimately, he decided that the only way he could make a living would be to set up a community arts organization and make himself the director of it. So, after spending some time driving around his home state of Minnesota, he happened upon New York Mills, a small town, population 972, where, with the help of a number of community grants, he managed to buy and fix up a large run-down building on Main Street and set up the New York Mills Cultural Center and Arts Retreat. Once settled, he turned the center into a hub of thriving activity, including musical performances, gallery exhibits, a retreat program for artists from across the country, and summer arts classes for children and adults.

Soon afterward, John got the idea to start the Great Midwestern Think-Off, a philosophy contest for ordinary people. John believed that there is much untapped wisdom outside of academia and wanted to create a showcase for it. The first Think-Off was held in 1993 when the final four contestants came to New York Mills, Minnesota, to defend their positions on the nature of humankind—is it inherently good or inherently evil? The competition was wildly successful and eventually became, in later years, the Great American Think-Off, an annual contest that attracts hundreds of entries from around the country.

Dave, who shares John Davis's view about the untapped philosophical wisdom of "nonphilosophers," has entered the contest nearly every year since its inception. In 2003, in keeping with a practice had he started a few years earlier, Dave integrated the Think-Off competition into his college-level teaching:

I had all the students in my winter-quarter Introduction to Philosophy class submit an entry as their final project. Because I wanted to model for them what I thought would be a viable entry, I wrote one, too, and submitted it, as well. The question for the 2003 competition was "Do You Reap What You Sow?"

In my essay, I argued that we don't reap what we sow, using several examples of failed attempts at gardening in my youth.

We held a Think-Off competition in my class. All papers were submitted and reviewed anonymously. I was delighted when mine was not chosen as a finalist; it warmed my heart as a teacher to see that the class thought their own papers were superior to mine, especially when it came out later that the national competition judges had selected my essay as one of the finalists.

Attending the Think-Off finals in New York Mills, Minnesota was a delight and, more importantly, a powerful reminder about the power of passion—what we care about—in our lives. The three other finalists and I were treated like royalty in the small town; we got to ride on a float in the annual Think-Off parade and be cheered all along the parade route. Some 400 people showed up at the town's gymnasium to hear us deliver our essays and debate the topic. No special effects, no car crashes, just individuals standing at a podium sharing their beliefs. One of the finalists, Arthur Yuwiler, was a 76-year-old retired biochemist. Arthur is truly a new elder. In the years since retirement, he has cultivated an interest in drawing, painting, and wood sculpture. But most prominently, he has cultivated his lifelong interest in creative thinking and writing. His passion for ideas was infectious and we found ourselves, all weekend long, having great conversations with him on all sorts of subjects. Seeing him up on stage, as he delivered his very moving essay in which he argued, drawing on the tragic example of his autistic grandson, that we do not reap what we sow, one could really see the boy in the man. The sharing of ideas that he cared about brought him alive in a way that few other activities could have.

While the audience for the Think-Off was mostly older folks, there were plenty of teenagers and young kids, too. And this, I think, is the real message of the Think-Off. It reminds us of the hunger that people of all ages have for passionate ideas. We're captivated by serious inquiry into serious matters. We want answers to the questions that really matter.

Or, to put it another way, we feel a powerful need to be around the fire and hear what those who have claimed their place have to say.

New Elder
Marilyn Whitcomb

Marilyn's story is far from unique—but it is, at least in part, the very typicality of her story that makes it so poignant. A stay-at-home mom for 25 years, Marilyn found herself in her late 40s facing the predictable challenges associated with the empty nest when the last of her three kids went off to college.

Marilyn spent some time redecorating her house, doing volunteer work, and catching up on her gardening, but it wasn't enough. She felt she needed something more, something she was really passionate about.

Marilyn reflected on what she cared most deeply about. She recalled how much she loved her English classes in high school and college and thought about all the novels that had meant so much to her over the years. "I'd always loved reading," she said, "books are one of the things that carried me through all the years. All the time I was raising my kids, books were my solace; when times were tough, I always had a book to read."

"When I was in school, though, I never thought it was practical to study English; it seemed like a luxury for kids who had money or trust funds. That's what's so inspiring about what I'm doing now; maybe it won't easily lead to some sort of job, but I'm studying what I really care about."

Marilyn is a graduate student in the Comparative Literature department at the University of Washington. At 52, she's twice as old as many of her fellow grads, but that doesn't faze her a bit. "That just gives me twice as much perspective on the readings as they have," she laughs. "Plus, some of the writers we read—like Saul Bellow or Norman Mailer—writers they think are 'old guys,' I consider my contemporaries. That gives me special insight into them that the other students don't have."

Marilyn isn't sure where her studies are going to take her. "I'm two years into a Ph.D. program that usually takes people eight to ten years. That means I might be 60 by the time I'm done. I guess I could be worried about that, but I'm not. Right now, I'm doing what I love—studying, writing about, and, as a graduate teaching assistant, instructing others—in literature. In eight years I'll be 60 whether I do this or not. So, there's nothing to be lost by doing it and everything—including my heartfelt passion—by not."

Old Dogs and New Tricks

One of the common barriers to growth and fulfillment in the second half is the notion that "it's too late." This is false. As long as what we're striving for is personal mastery—as opposed to say, Olympic Team membership—it's never too late.

Dave remembers talking to his friend's mother when he

was a mere lad of 16. He was telling her about how he had just begun learning to play the flute. "Oh," she said, with an implied reference to her own son, who began taking piano lessons at age 4, "you're sort of a Johnny-come-lately to music, aren't you?"

At 16 years old, a Johnny-come-lately? Hardly. Perhaps a 16-year-old who takes up a musical instrument may be too late to be a child prodigy, but he certainly is far from too late to develop a real expertise with the instrument and derive great satisfaction from playing it the rest of his life.

Same goes for someone at 50. Or 60. Or 70 or even 80. While it's true that, when we're younger, it tends to be easier to learn new things, especially things like language, there's no reason we can't take up new things much later in life. Tolstoy famously began learning Greek in his 70s so he could read Homer in the original. World-renowned cellist Pablo Casals was quoted as saying the reason he continued diligent daily practice into his 90s was that he thought he was getting better. Millions of lesser known individuals have taken up new skills far into their most advanced years.

Many others, though, refrain from doing so, claiming, "Oh, I'm just too old to learn." And while it is true that few over-50s will ever learn to shred some gnarly skateboard moves on a vertical pipe, any number of avenues of learning are open to people of any age.

The real challenge is to be able to look ahead and imagine that you will be able to learn what you set out to. At 16, this is pretty easy. We can forecast how good we'll be at the flute or guitar or French in ten years, at age 26. At 50, it seems harder to predict our success by age 60. But it shouldn't be. Ten years is still ten years; there's no particular reason (other than the difficulties of making time for new things in our later years) why we shouldn't be able to make as much progress at something from ages 50 to 60 as at ages 16 to 26. Moreover, by age 50, we should have two additional advantages. First, we will presumably have gained all sorts of perspectives that we didn't have as young people. We will understand our learning styles better; we'll have learned how to learn in new and more effective ways. Also, we'll have had loads more experience in what time means. At age 16, for example, ten years is an eternity. The very idea of sticking with something for a decade seems hardly conceivable. At age 50 or higher, ten years seems like a fairly small amount of time. The idea that we'll spend a decade practicing the guitar, or yoga, or learning Greek turns out to sound quite manageable. Like Woody Allen says, "I have ties older than that."

New Elder
Dr. Alvin P. Shapiro

Dave says: From a professional standpoint, my dad, Dr. Alvin P. Shapiro, had done it all. A physician, a full professor on the medical faculty at the University of Pittsburgh, he had achieved the highest possible status in his profession and won the abiding respect of colleagues throughout academia and the scientific community. In his over 30-year association with the university, he had held a number of impressive positions, including Dean of Students for the Medical School and Chairman of the Department of Medicine. Now, at age 65, he was entering the period of his career at which many of his colleagues tended to sit back and let the accolades roll in. He could pursue his own "pet projects" and, being a highly respected tenured professor, no one would dare raise an eyebrow against him. Moreover, having had open-heart surgery just a few years earlier, who could possibly begrudge the good doctor if he slowed down a bit? Wouldn't it be only natural for him to gradually disengage himself from the day-to-day dramas of the medical school world?

Natural, perhaps, but not at all what my dad had chosen to do. Whereas many of his medical contemporaries were reducing their clinic hours and beginning to work on their memoirs, Al was diving headfirst into a new project, a new hospital, a whole new class of medical students who faced challenges quite a bit different than the fairly privileged young doctors he had worked with at the University of Pittsburgh.

At age 65, my dad had chosen to take on the task of directing the Medicine Training Program at Shadyside Hospital, a teaching hospital in Pittsburgh whose doctors and patients were far more diverse than those across town at his former job. A good portion of the young residents he would now be working with were immigrants to the United States. There were graduates from medical schools in India, Pakistan, Russia, and Grenada, along with those from many smaller schools throughout the United States. The patients at Shadyside Hospital, too, tended to represent a broad swath of social, cultural, and economic differences. A local hospital whose reputation, though solid, was not quite as impressive as the Presbyterian Hospital at the University of Pittsburgh, Shadyside Hospital served a community more representative of Pittsburgh's population than its crosstown medical center.

So why was Dad doing this? Why was he choosing to blaze a new career path when he could have easily been resting on his laurels?

The answer is given in a humorous quote that my dad shared with me at the time: "Illegitimi non carborundum." This made-up Latin phrase means "Don't let the bastards grind you down." Dad explained to me that the medical teaching profession, at least as it was being conducted at the university at that time, was quite a bit different than what had originally drawn him to it. His passion was in helping young medical students to become real doctors—healers—who were dedicated to combining the best science possible with the most authentically human response to patients. He said that he felt some schools overemphasized technological solutions that did little to train students in what they really needed to assist patients.

He told me a story about how one of his younger colleagues at his former school instructed some residents in diagnostic techniques using a computer-based artificial-intelligence expert system. While not at all a neo-Luddite (my dad was one of the first physicians he knew who owned a computer; in his 50s, he even taught himself some programming), he nevertheless found it odd that the students weren't being shown the simple method that allowed a physician like himself to successfully diagnose the patient's condition from a five-minute examination of his eye movements and skin tone.

Plus, he also wanted to work with more students who, like himself, had come to the medical profession from rather modest backgrounds. A son of a shopkeeper on Staten Island, New York, Dad had few financial or cultural advantages to help him succeed in his profession. Many students at the larger medical schools were sons or daughters of physicians—they had all the help they needed. At Shadyside, though, my dad felt he could give his students the sort of opportunities he had to make something of themselves.

The transitions my dad was facing weren't going to be easy; he faced a new setting, new colleagues, new responsibilities, even a new commute from home. But facing those transitions was, he believed, the very thing that gave his professional—and by extension, his personal—life meaning. As he explained to me, he was far too old to have to do any of this, but far too young not to.

Keeping Hope Alive

We want to make a connection between a renewed sense of calling and a renewed sense of hope. One of the most common—and most tragic—complaints of people in the second half of life is that they've "lost hope." This is quite understandable. When we feel alienated from our stories or our sense of place or, most importantly, a feeling of passion about what we're doing, it's not surprising that we would feel somewhat hopeless.

But what is hope? The American Heritage Dictionary defines it as "A wish or desire accompanied by confident expectation of its fulfillment." So, there are two elements: the wish and the expectation.

To wish for something is to aspire to it. *Aspire* comes from the Latin root meaning "breathe," which is also connected to the word for spirit. The breath, in many theological traditions, is intimately a part of spirit. *Prana,* for instance, the life force in the Hindu tradition, is synonymous with the breath. Or *chi,* in Chinese theology and medicine, also has its source in the breath. For that matter, the Holy Spirit in Christianity is often associated with the breath.

To hope, then, is in a very real manner of speaking, to breathe. We all know, for instance, that when we're scared or anxious or depressed—when we lose hope—how difficult it is to get air into our lungs. And we know that one of the most effective ways to begin to re-center ourselves and overcome our fear, is to refocus upon and recover our breathing.

We can say, then, that keeping hope alive means to keep our breath alive. To hope is to breathe with the confident expectation of our ongoing fulfillment, to aspire for something better, to keep wishing that our all dreams will come true.

So how is this done in the second half of life? How do we keep hope alive when so much of what we have always hoped for—success at work, increased monetary rewards, improved health—may not be available to us?

The answer, we think, is somewhat paradoxical. Normally, we think of hope as a forward-looking emotion—and it is. But here, we want to conceive of the forward-looking as a kind of backward-looking, too.

What we mean by this is that our hope is not just for tomorrow but is also a kind of hope for the past. It is a hope for our own past—that the past we have lived has had a

meaning, has been for something, that we have made a difference in someone's life, not just our own.

Keeping this hope for the past alive involves taking stock
of our life and the choices we've made in it. It means looking
back over what we've done and thinking about how we've gotten where we are and why. This doesn't mean we should over-
analyze and get bogged down in regret—for none of us has
lived a life that couldn't be better—rather, it means we need
to reflect upon our choices in a manner that allows us to put
them in perspective. We have to take into account the circumstances under which we made those choices in the first place.
So, for instance, even though we may wish that "we knew then
what we know now," it's incumbent upon us to realize that
this just wasn't the case: We did the best we could with the
information we had. We can't change the past.

What we can do, however, is change the future based on
the past. And in this way, keep hope for tomorrow—and for
yesterday, as well—alive.

The key to hope is having something to look forward to.
And what's key to that is doing something that will potentially
bear fruit in the future. It's not enough to merely have some
outcome or event to anticipate; hope is not particularly
inspired simply by looking forward to the release of the next
Harry Potter book or Superbowl XLIII. Rather, hope is stimulated when the outcome or event we anticipate is something
we've contributed to. And it doesn't have to be something
great or earth-shattering; planting a vegetable garden will do.

That said, hope is most powerfully stimulated by taking
part in something that will bear fruit in the lives of others.
Sowing a vegetable garden is good; sowing a human garden is
even better.

Ask yourself: What am I hoping for? And which of these hopes involve me more directly in the lives of others? The outcomes whose success you contribute to are those that offer you the greatest potential for keeping the fire of hope burning most brightly—and in this way, reignite your passion for the second half of your life.

Fireside Chat
What Do I Care About?

This fireside chat encourages dialogue around how to renew our calling and reignite our passions by making connections with our youth. Ideally, this fireside chat would include a new elder and one or more younger people. If that's not possible, though, it can still be valuable and successful as a conversation between people of similar ages.

As always, the success of this fireside chat can be enhanced by creating an environment that draws upon the ancient power of the fire. If you can manage to set this up outside, around an actual fire, so much the better. If not, we really do encourage you to speak by candlelight if possible.

The Firestarter Question

What is the gift, lesson, or legacy you most want to pass on to those who follow you? Why?

Encourage all your fireside partners to contribute to the discussion. Speak your minds. Speak from the heart. Keep the fire of dialogue alive!

Tending the Fire

The Fire of Passion: What Do I Care About?

The word "enthusiasm" comes from the Greek, *enthousias-mos*—to be possessed—*en theos,* "in God." What are you enthusiastic or "in God" about?

Think of the new elders you know who have real enthusiasm about what they do. Think of those folks who are so passionate and committed to their vocation that you can hardly picture them doing anything else. What core characteristics do these new elders have in common?

Now get a copy of today's paper—or even better, the most recent Sunday paper. Review every single page: the news, editorials, features, sports, business, comics, society, entertainment, world and local events, want ads, even the obituaries. What things grab your attention? What themes or issues do you naturally migrate to? Highlight three things that really move you, about which you feel "Someone really needs to do something."

What most excites you in or about the world? What most angers you? What do you care about most deeply? If you could teach three things to others, what would you teach? Who would you teach it to?

"Nothing great was ever achieved without enthusiasm," wrote Emerson. A deep enthusiasm, especially for something undertaken with vitality and verve, is how even "unremarkable" people can achieve something remarkable. Enthusiasm is probably the one most common feature among the new elders we have interviewed for this book.

Enthusiasm is the active component of our life's passions. Passion is the fuel of which enthusiasm is the flame. Our passions are what keep the fire burning in the second half of life.

Renewing our calling, and so, reigniting our passions, enables us to spark our own enthusiasm and, just as importantly, the enthusiasm of young people. The actual stories we tell may be forgotten, but our living passion is an inspiring power.

Passion is inextricably linked to vital aging. New elders with a real zest for the second half of life draw upon their passions to keep them going while contemporaries are slumbering. They are passionately growing whole, not old.

Chapter 4

The Flame of Meaning

Reclaiming Our Purpose

New Elder

Frederic Hudson

"I refuse to become a marginalized person! So many people just disappear, lose their nerve, and disconnect. Not me. I'm at the end of who I was. But I'm at the beginning of who I might become. That's exciting to me."

These bold reflections from Frederic Hudson opened his dialogue with Richard on a sunny May morning in Santa Barbara, California. As the sunlight slanted through the living room windows of the Hudson household, Frederic took Richard on a passionate journey through his recent paintings. As he spoke, he was describing—as someone who is coming to terms with the onset of Alzheimer's disease—what it is like to confront the limitations of the flesh.

"I've had to give up one era of my life," Frederic claims, "in order to enter another. I've always been fascinated with how people deconstruct and reconstruct their lives. We all need to constantly do this, to reinvent ourselves."

Frederic speaks slowly, crisply, and clearly. This friend and colleague of Richard, this new elder who one year ago worked with a vengeance—traveling, speaking, writing and creating, always creating. Frederic, founder of both the Fielding and Hudson Institutes, is one of the thought leaders in adult development and coaching in America. Today Frederic savors solitude. "The life force," he says, "now is about celebrating life and about generosity—giving it all away. It's all about being. The peace I'm gaining is coming from using my illness as a challenge, as permission to be."

Frederic uses his affliction as a new calling to confront the larger human condition. He's matter of fact about his disease. He says, "I don't call it Alzheimer's. I call it some kind of brain thing. My situation is only a particular type of what we all face," he says, "for we all live in bodies that are imperfect."

Richard reflects, "Suddenly I find myself confronting a great paradox. I see before me the possibility of all that Frederic may lose. But the mystery lies in what remains. What is clearly evident in Frederic is "the defiant power of the human spirit"—the stuff of life that our mutual teacher, Viktor Frankl, modeled and espoused." Why are we so obsessed with what we lose as we age, and unclear about what we gain?

"Just doing things now, for their own sake, is enough," claims Frederic. "I'm living for the sake of the songs in my heart and giving any service I can render."

Frederic is finding meaning in his suffering, facing his condition like another calling. He is reversing an entire illness stereotype along with all the habits of thought that perpetuate it. Why does it seem that so few people are endowed with this defiant power—the courage to face suffering without embarrassment?

Frederic relates, "This condition has minimized my impact and changed my outer world identity. It has given me a new permission to be. It has allowed me time to speak with flowers, trees, birds, and my dogs." In his daily routines now, he engages in as much nonverbal expression as possible. He feels less need to be with people to feel good. He feels liberated from talking, writing, and working. "This is ultimate cocooning," he says. "I can go for walks, paint, compose, play the piano, and garden. I've always been an experimenter with new ideas and this solitude is new for me. I'm reviewing a book a day and I paint every day. I plan to keep writing some and sharing my views on this process."

Recently, while looking for something else, Frederic started recycling his vast library of books to places he felt would like them. "Clearing those shelves heartens me," he says. "In going through my books, I wanted to unearth some answers to this question: 'What do we need to become an elder?' Living in that question, I'm releasing all the ideas I no longer need, which is most of them. In all ways, I want to enter this elder phase of life carrying as little as possible—unpacking as you say. That way my mind, hands, and heart will be free to be."

What Frederic learned as a child was how to challenge the system; that's what wise elders taught him. They helped him move beyond the set limits of his upbringing. They helped him create his own future scenarios.

"Adelaide Mead, my 70-year-old mentor when I was a child, was a radical socialist and painter in my Baptist church," he recalls. "She was totally alive. When I was 15, I would visit her to learn her ways. She adopted me. She always inquired of me, 'How is your life shaping up? You need to go to college and get out of here!' At the time I was attending a vocational high school to become a manual laborer, a tradesman. She kept telling me, 'You have gifts beyond this town.'"

For over 30 years, Frederic has been a student of elderhood. "Most elders are not about wisdom," he claims. "They haven't earned the right to be considered wise. To earn the right, you have to know yourself, know your boundaries, know your gifts—and then be generous. I used to call retirement protirement. But I was wrong. There's no tirement at all. In elderhood you're more a human being than a human doing. Elderhood is just another calling."

Richard left his interview with Frederic in a mood of high alert. He saw that purpose is giving sense and meaning to the changes in Frederic's life. Purpose is a therapeutic idea. Frederic is living for the sake of the songs in his heart. Richard relates, "I saw the power of purpose on display in his style, habit, gesture, mood, and presence. His face reveals purpose and appeals to purpose. His new mantra, *permission to be,* reveals an example of another calling."

Frederic, like many of the new elders we interviewed for this book, takes pain to stress that he is proud of being an elder, not ashamed. He is proud, in spite of his challenges, of the deepening of his creativity and the ripening of his soul that would have been impossible in his earlier years. For

Frederic, as for us, learning how to live has gone hand in hand with learning how to age.

Theodore Roszak's book, *America the Wise,* looks forward to the age of wisdom and to the triumph of elderhood. The sheer number of elders could revolutionize society to what Roszak calls, "the survival of the gentlest." Frederic is furthering Roszak's vision by being a gentle revolutionary.

And these days, could there be any revolution more revolutionary than gentleness?

Retiring from Retirement

The book, *About Schmidt,* by Louis Begley, upon which the movie is based, has other insights into retirement than those explored in the film. In one passage, Schmidt's oldest friend, Gil, chastises Schmidt for his decision to retire.

"I told you to take a leave for as long as necessary after Mary, and not even think of retiring. There is a race of men— all federal and state and bank employees, and most dentists— who are born to retire. They aspire to retirement from the moment they are born. Youth, sex, work, are only the necessary intermediate states: progresses from larva to pupa to nymph until, at last, the miracle of metamorphosis is complete and gives the world the retired butterfly. Golf clubs, funny shoes, and designer sunglasses for the dentist, campers and gas-fired barbecue sets for the employees at the low end of the pay scale! You and I belong to a grander race. We need to be kneaded by misfortune and modern medicine before we are ready. Praised be to the Lord, I am happy to announce that you strike me as unripe for a living death. What you need is a job. I'm going to think one up for you."

We would take Gil's admonition one step further: As far as we're concerned, no one, even the dentists and state workers, is fit for retirement. Retirement is an artificial concept and one that for new elders is becoming obsolete.

What is retirement for, anyway? When we grow old, how exactly do we grow? Why do we hear so much about "staying" young and so little about growing old?

Because we have grown up in such a youth-driven culture, we face both an opportunity and a danger as we consider retiring. The opportunity clearly is that we can look and feel and act younger than our parents' generation. The danger, however, is that we will shun the value and meaning of aging. Popular culture reveals a deep denial about aging, a denial far deeper than our wrinkles. Even our aging comics are in denial when it comes to aging. Bill Cosby, in his bestseller, *Time Flies,* draws a gloomy self-portrait of aging by deciding that he needs help "either from a divinity or a drugstore." Page after page Cosby laments the passing of his athletic prowess and the arrival of his paunch.

Stripped of its humor, this is our culture's general wisdom about aging: Resist it at all costs! In writing the book *Age Wave,* Dr. Ken Dycthwald was shocked at how deep our anti-aging bias is. He "quickly learned something very interesting about how Americans want to think about aging: they don't."

Caught up in the eternal quest to stay young, we are unaware of the growth and transcendence possible in the second half of life. As Stephen Levine writes in his book *Who Dies?* "We live in a strange land where one is punished for being old."

In our study of new elders, we are struck by the similarity between what happens around retirement and what happens to those who experience "near-death experiences." After undergoing calamities like September 11, 2001, or accidents that brought them to the edge of life, people report value shifts in their lives that are similar to many experiencing retirement. During profound transitions people go "higher" and they go "deeper" in their experience of life.

They go higher in terms of their appreciation for nature and the beauty and interconnectedness of all life. They go deeper in terms of renewing their relationship with God or a spiritual presence in their lives. Together, they claim a generally height-ened awareness of the spiritual purpose and meaning of life.

In his 30s Richard began his studies of elders, and he read Ernest Becker's Pulitzer prize-winning book, *The Denial of Death*. He recalls, "I was fascinated with what Becker called 'the real dilemma of existence, the one of the mortal animal who at the same time is conscious of his mortality.'"

At the same time he read Becker's work, Richard attended a program by the eminent death and dying expert, Elizabeth Kübler-Ross and something clicked. Kübler-Ross's stages of dying, starting with denial (stage 1) and ending with accep-tance (stage 5) come only after deep, often painful transfor-mation experiences that fit perfectly with Richard's observation of his life and the lives of his coaching clients. Learning about the process of death seemed to be an essen-tial part of all life transitions, as well as of growing up.

The Wisdom of the Body

Fifty-four years ago, psychologist Rollie Larson's body spoke to him with considerable authority. He didn't listen. After all, he was on a fast track to "success" as he envisioned it.

So why should he slow down when things were going so well when he was an active, healthy young man? Result: a severe case of pneumonia—misdiagnosed, leading to a lengthy hospital stay, saving his life with 49 penicillin shots and lots of rest. Such inactivity gave him an opportunity to learn a bit about what his body was trying to tell him.

Little by little during the next few years Rollie began asking himself the big questions: "Who am I, really? Where am I going? Is this all there is? If not, what else is out there? Do I trust this inner voice that seems to nudge me at times? Do I need to keep pursuing the same old things on the job, duties that are increasingly repetitive and boring? Who's in charge, anyhow?"

It was a time when he had reached many of his career goals, with little challenge left. At age 46 he was (unknowingly) ripe for change. But he had not really considered changing his job because it represented everything he wanted: adequate compensation, security, recognition, use of his talents, great working conditions, and wonderful colleagues. But something was missing. Rollie recalls, "I knew it and I didn't know it. My life was just too busy, living the whole success lifestyle of a public school supervisor."

It was a time when, in many ways, Rollie was at his peak. His department had just been commended as a "model for the nation" by a team of educators sent from Washington to learn what he was doing and how he did it. With all of this happening it seemed there was no logical reason to change his vocation.

It was a time, however, when his body was sending messages that he was slow to pick up. He recalls, "In retrospect I now see things more clearly. I was tired a great deal, yawned a lot, and often had tight feelings in my chest. Periodic chest pains would accelerate during times of tension from work-related problems."

It was also a time when a friend encouraged Rollie to join him in a pioneering effort in a small, start-up nonprofit organization. His encouragement made it sound possible and exciting. Rollie said, "For the first time I realized I could not spend another 20 years where I was. I felt boxed in, trapped, and hadn't realized it."

Rollie wanted badly to take the new position, but he also needed the security features of his present job. He would need to give up his accelerating pension plan, 120 days of accumulated sick leave, and other fringe benefits for a job that was grant-funded for only three years. He would also take a salary cut of 30 percent to leave what he had considered to be his ideal job. He recalls, "It seemed crazy to give up all of this with four kids in school, ages 11 to 17 and a wife not employed outside of the home. We had no savings!"

Fortunately, Rollie's wife, Doris, was there to listen and help him clarify. They grew closer, and he began to realize that security in the conventional sense did not mean everything. He began to experience a feeling of freedom and control of his future. Security took on new meaning. "Security," Rollie learned, "is largely within me."

Rollie felt more alive than he had in a long time. Continuing to develop his talents made him feel as if life were beginning again. He felt younger, yet unsure and self-doubting at times. He recalls, "I was certain that the choice to leave my secure position was the right one. It was as if Goethe had written these lines for me: whatever you can do or dream you can do, begin it. Boldness has genius, power and magic in it."

The decision Rollie made at age 46 eventually led to opportunities that he could never have imagined. Working alongside a highly creative colleague in an exciting, challenging career was followed, seven years later, by Rollie, and his wife Doris, going into private practice together. Prior to retiring they conducted over 800 workshops and seminars worldwide and co-authored four books.

In retrospect, now at age 82, new elder Rollie claims, "Within my heart is a feeling of deep gratitude. It is like a priceless gift was given to me as I trusted a spiritual process of growth at a critical juncture of life. Doris and I learned that honest communication, listening, and risk taking are our best friends. I cringe when I think of the opportunities and life satisfaction we might have missed if we had not 'just done it' at age 46!"

"At 82," says Rollie, "it's easy to lose your motivation. My purpose keeps me motivated. Sun City turns me off. I don't want to spend all my time with old people. Keeping a youthfulness (and mentoring youth) is critical to me. Working out brings me to life! And giving something away brings me to life. I don't want to hold onto stuff anymore. If there is joy in giving, I want to give it now. A lot of people give money and things away, but the ultimate contribution is giving of yourself. My purpose is to give myself now, through deep listening. 'Listen to someone today!' has been and still is my daily mantra."

Purpose is not a matter of theology. Our beliefs about the hereafter are not what ultimately matter. What matters is whether we live out our beliefs. Or as Stephen Levine puts it in *Who Dies?*: "Death is not the enemy. The enemy is ignorance and lovelessness."

The reason why the issue of purpose is so important to a vital second half of life is that it raises issues that, ultimately, are inevitable. None of us is going to get out of this life without facing the question "Why am I here?" None of us is going to be able to avoid confronting the question of our life's meaning. We don't really get away with not wondering what our legacy will be after we're gone.

By thinking intentionally about our life's purpose—by thoughtfully reflecting on our life's meaning—we give ourselves the time and space to think about things that sooner or later we're going to have to think about, whether we want to or not. And if we do this well and do it with intention, we can define our life's purpose and reclaim it so that we are able to integrate it successfully in all that we do throughout the second half of our lives. New elders do this and do so in ways that make their lives more vital for themselves and for family, friends, and, in many cases, clients and customers as well.

New Elder
Cal Wick

American industry spends 31 billion dollars a year on corporate education. The problem, though, is that few people who attend corporate training courses actually apply what they learn. All their good intentions to put into practice what they've learned in seminars, trainings, and workshops quickly evaporate once they are back on the job.

Cal Wick, the 60-year-old CEO of Fort Hill Company in Montchanin, Delaware, recognized this problem and has built a business in response to it.""Creating new ways to help people learn how to do important things is how I define my purpose." Cal has turned his purpose into a profitable enterprise in the second half of his life. He is passionate about the things that Fort Hill is doing as an expression of that purpose to help transform companies such as Pfizer, Home Depot, and Hewlett-Packard.

Cal, a former Episcopalian priest, is a new elder. Like the other new elders who appear on the pages of this book, he has life lessons to teach us.

Cal takes pains to stress that he is proud of being well into the second half of life; it's not at all something he is ashamed of, recoils from, or is afraid to admit. He is proud of the deepening of his emotions and the ripening of his faith that would have been impossible even five years earlier. He says, "I'm in roles that I've never had before. At times, I wake up with wisdom that was previously inaccessible to me—I'm like a child learning to speak." For Cal, learning how to lead has gone hand in hand with learning how to age.

In our interviews with new elders, we were struck by the similarities between what happens as we approach the second half of life and what happens to those who survive near-death experiences. After undergoing medical emergencies or accidents that brought them close to death, people report major changes in their lives and attitudes about living. These major changes include a deeper sense of purpose and a fuller appreciation for the interconnectedness of all life.

At age 59, Cal found that he had potential throat cancer and was losing his voice. This awareness of his mortality penetrated deeply into his consciousness. He says that as a direct result of this experience, "I feel much more open about saying what's on my mind. Having cancer you know that you don't know how much time you have left. It causes you to wrestle with your faith."

While passing by a San Francisco bookstore several years ago, he saw a book about honoring the Sabbath and it changed his life. "I was working flat-out seven days a week and I was fried." Today, Cal Wick lives out his beliefs through his own "Sabbath practices."

Cal reports that, for him, Saturday and Sunday are both Sabbath days. He says, "In my prayers from Friday to Sunday, I only give thanks. I spend no money on Sundays. Through this practice, a real sense of gratitude has emerged. It slows me down enough to listen. Sometimes prayers come to me which I put on my website: www.greatprayers.com. The book of Genesis talks about time being holy. My Sabbath practice connects my living with eternity."

People who are living on purpose during the second half of life like Cal Wick are not drifting quietly onto the golf course but are using their gifts, purpose, and passion in service to others. For Cal, this means not only running a purposeful organization but also serving through preaching four or five times a year, plus doing weddings and coaching people through difficult life transitions. As Cal demonstrates, the gift of the second half of life is fully appreciated only when it is shared.

The Freedom to Choose

According to adult development researchers, the epiphanies that followed a taste of their mortality for people like Frederic Hudson, Rollie Larson, and Cal Wick happened right on schedule. In the second half of life, this awareness of mortality shifts our perspective and opens our eyes to the deep and vulnerable wonders of the sacred. Whether this awareness will be a negative or a positive force, one that undermines life's purpose or enriches it, is up to each of us. It's our choice whether we will draw strength from life's challenges or be defeated by them.

Or is it?

Are we truly free to live the second half of our lives on purpose?

In every situation we find ourselves in, we have the freedom of deciding for or against the influence of our surroundings. Viktor Frankl, in a moving description of inmates of the concentration camps during World War II describes examples of men and women who, under the most adverse circumstances, were able to "do differently," to choose to care for others, in a situation in which every other external human freedom was denied.

Frankl describes this in *Man's Search for Meaning:* "Probably in every concentration camp," he reports, "there were individuals who were able to overcome their apathy and suppress their irritability. These were the ones who were examples of renunciation and self-sacrifice. Asking nothing for themselves, they went about in the grounds and in the barracks of the camp offering a kind word here, a crust of bread there."

From them we learn that freedom is not something we "have," and therefore can lose, it is what we "are." It is our deepest potential, only needing to be embraced.

The notion of reclaiming our purpose is not new—the essential questions facing us have not really changed over time. What is new, at least to some extent, is the degree of freedom we now have in the second half of life to develop our own answers.

Virtually everyone we interviewed for this book referred to some event that heightened awareness of their mortality. During the second half of life, purpose is on our minds, and it should be.

New Elder
Dr. Jeffrey Life

Growing older is a fact of life; if we're not growing older, then we're not living. How we feel about the process of aging profoundly influences our experience in the second half of life. Is getting older a blessing or a curse? Do we see it as a decline or an ascent? Do we resist it at every turn or welcome it into our life? Our answers to these questions are critical because in the second half of life, they shape our destiny.

For Jeffrey Life, M.D., at age 58, aging was a curse. Going through a traumatic divorce left him emotionally and physically exhausted, and his relationship with his daughter seemed ruined. He recalls, "My self-esteem had

never been lower, my waist never bigger, and my choles-
terol never higher. It was time to get my life under
control."

Jeff started exercising and setting goals. His patients
asked him what he was doing to look so healthy. His
friends couldn't get over his transformation. More importantly, his relationship with his teenage daughter began to
flourish. They even exercised together!

Jeff signed up for the "Body for Life" program—and
won it at age 60! Through this 12-week personal transformation program, he became fascinated with exercise,
nutrition, and longevit. He began to incorporate "age-
management" principles, along with his own experience,
into his medical practice.

Today, he says, "I look at myself and I feel a sense of
pride. I really like what I see. I'm reminded of the Bob
Seger song: 'Lean and Solid Everywhere—Like a Rock.'
Only I'm not 18 years old as he was—I'm over 65!"

Behind Jeff's story of mid-life transformation—ending
addictions, losing weight, building strength—is a common
pattern. He was fed up with the way he had lived in the
first half of life and wanted to make changes in the second. He was seeking deeper grounding in himself—a new
purpose. "Deep self-renewal," writes Roger Gould in *Transformations,* "is not just a mental goal. It is so deep that we
cannot grasp its origins with the mind alone."

Dr. Alex Comfort once reflected that only 25 percent
of what we call "aging" is rooted in the actual biology of
being older. The other 75 percent of aging he called
"sociogenic"—that is, caused by stereotypes, myths, and

misconceptions that society and culture impose on older adults.

As Jeff faced the second half of his life, he confronted a critical choice about his purpose. What, he wondered, was his life all about? What was the legacy he was leaving? The answers to those questions helped him structure his choices.

Five years ago, he attended an "anti-aging" medical meeting. He heard from a company called Cenegenics Medical Institute about three other aspects of the anti-aging program: nutrition, exercise, and hormone modulation. Coming fresh on the heels of his victory in the "Body for Life" contest, this information launched him on a new direction in his medical practice for the second half of his life.

Today, in addition to his M.D. in Internal Medicine, he has a Ph.D. in Nutrition and a black belt in karate. Certified in Age-Management Medicine, he works as Institute Physician for Cenegenics Medical Institute in Las Vegas, Nevada, helping to keep people at the highest levels of wellness possible for as long as possible. He even writes a Performance Nutrition column for *Muscle Magazine's* 500,000 readers.

Jeff's purpose in the second half of life is helping people sustain youthfulness as they age. "My goal," he relates, "is to die young at a very old age!" To achieve this, he heads to the gym at five AM five days a week. He works out with training partners half his age. He says, "It energizes me for the whole day. It helps me to stay fit for the stressful life of a physician in this day and age. By not being encumbered by ill health, I'm physically free to do what I want to do!"

Traditional medicine doesn't pay a lot of attention to age management, Jeff claims. "How we see aging, and how our society sees it, is a question that goes to the very heart of claiming your place at the fire. New elders will face the choice of not just whether or when, but HOW to search for that elusive fountain of youth."

Talking to Our Ancestors

One of the things that inevitably happens as we age is that we get closer and closer to those who came before us. As we move into the years of the people who represented elder wisdom for us, we quite literally draw closer and closer to them spiritually and emotionally. "Every year," says Dave, "I hear and feel the presence of my father, my grandfathers, and my grandmothers more deeply. I really believe that, as I edge closer to the edge of my own life, I am gradually entering into their realm of wisdom. Each year, I'm more and more able to communicate with them, through a deeper connection to something within me."

As far out as this may sound, it's a common experience of elders. Moving into the second half of our lives, we move more closely into the circle of our ancestors. The fullest expression of this is that, in some sense, we develop the ability to communicate with anyone who has ever lived. We develop the ability to talk to anyone who ever lived.

In the heartbreakingly beautiful novel, *The Lovely Bones,* by Alice Seybold, heaven is a place where those who have died can look down on the living and watch us all the time. We need not take this literally in any sense nor require a change in our deeply held spiritual beliefs to feel the pull of Seybold's metaphor: Everyone who ever loved us, even a little bit, is up in heaven watching over us. The closer we get to our own journey to heaven—whatever that means for us— the more we are able to connect with those dear ones who have been attending to our progress through life from above.

Claiming our place at the fire, then, is in some sense, joining into the circle of heavenly watchers. Our role becomes more and more to be a conduit for their wisdom to those who need it here on Earth.

As we age, most of us, in some way, get more in touch with the spiritual nature of our existence. As our bodies decline, it's only natural that we should be drawn to aspects of life that are less ephemeral, more eternal.

For some people, this turning toward spirituality manifests itself in a return or reconnection to the spiritual practices of their earlier lives. For others, this emerging spirituality leads them to seek other practices in new or more esoteric traditions.

Whatever your theological or spiritual bent, be it atheist to devout theist, you will do well in the second half to find new ways to attune to your spiritual side. This wellspring of emerging spirituality becomes a source of greater power and fulfillment. It becomes an important font of creative expression and connection with friends, family members, and the community at large. It becomes, in short, another way to claim our place at the fire.

Fireside Chat
Reclaiming Our Purpose

This fireside chat encourages dialogue around how to reclaim our purpose and communicate that sense of purpose to others. Ideally, this fireside chat would involve a group with a variety of spiritual perspectives. If that's not possible, though, it can still be valuable and successful as a conversation between just a couple of people.

The Firestarter Question

Ask yourself: "For the sake of what am I living in the second half of my life?"

With the answer to that question in mind, write a clear statement of your purpose. Answer the question, "For the sake of what?" and you have the essence of your purpose. It's an easy question to ask, but a demanding one to answer. It's a lifetime question. Purpose has a spiritual core; at our core, we are spiritual beings.

Once you've identified your purpose, have a fireside chat about it.. Encourage your fireside partners to contribute to the discussion. Speak your minds. Speak from the heart. Keep the fire of dialogue alive!

Tending the Fire
The Flame of Meaning: What Is My Purpose?

In our earlier book, *Repacking Your Bags,* we reported that research shows that people's number one deadly fear is the fear of "having lived a meaningless life." Naming one's purpose can help us overcome this fear and, as such, is perhaps the most critical activity in which we can engage in the second half of life.

A purpose statement is, in essence, a written-down reason for being. As such, a purpose statement can be used to initiate, evaluate, and refine nearly all of our choices in life.

In John Gardner's book, *The Art of Living,* a character says, "The thing a person's gotta have—a human being—is some kind of center to his life, some one thing he's good at that other people need from him, like, for instance, shoemaking. I mean something ordinary, but at the same time holy, if you know what I mean."

What is at the center of your life? Did you discover "something ordinary but at the same time holy?" as a driving force in the first half of life? Do you have it to carry you forward in the second half of your life?

One of the first questions to ask yourself in naming your purpose is: *When have I been willing to commit myself to something beyond the scope of my own self-interest?* When, in other words, have I been at least as focused on the needs of others as my own? That willingness has to be there; it is a necessary condition of living on purpose. When we are acting with purpose, our life is never quite entirely our own. We are giving of it rather than getting for it. Acting purposefully, we find ourselves using our gifts in the service of something bigger than or outside of ourselves.

In spite of the power of living on purpose, most people find it rather difficult to craft a statement of personal purpose. Fortunately, a few techniques can help you render an initial purpose statement that then can be modified over time.

When Richard first developed his purpose statement, it was broad and encompassed many activities. Subsequently, it has become simpler and more straightforward, more of an affirmation that says, "This is what I am about."

We cannot fully name our purpose until we know ourselves—our spiritual nature, what we stand for, our emotional core. And yet this knowledge inevitably emerges as we put words to our purpose and refine them throughout our lives. Richard currently defines his purpose as "to uncover and inspire divine callings." Dave identifies his as "fostering understanding." Both of these have undergone a series of changes and we continue to look over, revise, and reclaim them as we age and grow.

As a spark for naming your own purpose, begin by looking over the following list of verbs. Pick the three that resonate most powerfully within you. These are the action verbs that will shape your purpose statement.

awaken   ignite   organize   create   teach   support
empower   develop   accept   encourage   help
listen   inspire   seek   design   enhance
challenge   act upon   learn   heal   energize

Write down your three choices.

Now, in just a few words, write down the answer to these questions: "What do I stand for? What is my core?"

Combine that answer with one or more of the verbs you have chosen. This is your draft purpose statement for now.

How do you feel when you look at it? Say it aloud. Does it fit? Would others agree that it fits you? Are you enthusiastic about it?

Is there anything more important in the second half of life than directing ourselves in accordance with our true purpose? George Bernard Shaw wrote:

"This is the true joy in life, the being used for a purpose recognized by yourself as a mighty one; the being thoroughly worn out before you are thrown on the scrap heap; the being a force of Nature instead of a feverish little clod of ailments and grievances complaining that the world will not devote itself to making you happy."

Ultimately, it is not so much a matter of *finding* a purpose that gives us such true joy as it is a matter of *recognizing* what our purpose already is and *claiming* it. And when we are able to claim it—and live it—we will have taken what is perhaps the most important step of all to growing whole, not old, in the second half of life.

Keeping the Fire Alive

Claim Your Place At the Fire

There are at least three times in life when we ought to be required to go off on a retreat to sit by a fire and reflect on the next stage of our lives. One is when we choose our vocation, another is when we choose a life partner, and the third is when we contemplate retirement. Something happens to us when we sit before fires. New feelings come up within us, and new visions come into our eyes that were not there before. A fire shifts the mood to one of purpose and possibility. No matter where a fire happens to be, it always weaves its spell.

At one time in our history, fires were our homes. We slept circled around them at night. We gathered for councils. Around fires, lives of hope are created and unwritten vows are made, which differ little from our ancestors. Around the fire we feel a sense of our place in the universe. And we feel the whole world is our home and all who are gathered are our partners on life's journey.

Once we feel the warmth and connections around a fire, we make contact with our stories and with the universal stories of our ancestors. So core is this feeling that even the building of a fire has symbolic significance. Each step in building a fire evokes our stories. Although we may not need the fire today for warmth or cooking, it is still a human necessity.

It gives us an opportunity to participate in a sacred act. The fire is a living thing.

Whenever humans have been on the move, the fire at day's end has always been the goal—a place of gratitude and reflection. No matter the era, this has remained true—our ancient needs for fire are still very much alive. Keeping the fire alive is essential to the magic of living on purpose. It helps us to feel part of an ongoing, ancient story, an evolutional act. The fire serves as a benediction to the adventures of the day and ultimately of a purposeful life.

When you go to the villages of indigenous peoples, like the hunter-gatherer Hadza in East Africa, and you participate in that most elemental of human experiences—sitting around a fire at night, talking, trading stories, sharing wisdom—you come to notice a certain arrangement of the group emerge naturally. Certain people find places closer to the fire; these members of the group tend to be the primary participants in the discussions and storytelling. Behind them tends to be a larger group—not excluded, but at a respectful distance—listening.

The spontaneous arrangement is determined in part by age, but more so, by wisdom. Those who have a wise voice to offer, those who from life experience, reflection, and choice, are sources of wisdom for their people are those who naturally claim a place close to the fire.

We view *new elders*—people living on purpose in the second half of their lives—as much like this. Becoming a new elder means finding one's voice and claiming one's right and responsibility to speak. And like the arrangement of individuals around the tribal campfire, it does not depend solely on a physical state like white hair or wrinkled skin. Rather, it is typified by states of minds and heart that are common to those upon whom we rely for guidance in the long term.

There is no universal path for becoming a new elder. But the four flames of vital aging we have explored in this book—identity, community, passion, and purpose—can help light the path.

Becoming a new elder is a choice: It's a way of relating to the world and the people in it that, though it generally bears a relationship to getting older, is neither guaranteed nor prevented by one's chronological state. It is characterized by a willingness and desire to continue deepening the experience of living, knowing that life is about ongoing development at every age. New elders recognize and accept their own mortality while still continuing to grow.

There is an evolving elder within each of us, and there is a danger of losing contact with that story in ourselves. As C. G. Jung put it, "Every human being has a two million-year-old man within himself, and if he loses contact with that two million-year-old self, he loses his real roots." The elder within is an essential part of our genetic hardwiring. When we cease growing, we die. And even if no one else notices the deadness in our souls, we notice.

Becoming a new elder means becoming a nurturer of life—human life and all life on the planet. It involves a kind of paradoxical power—one that comes from relinquishing external power but which requires us to take ownership of our internal power. It means claiming our voice, speaking softly, yet with conviction and strength.

The archetypal elder has been the critical force in most cultures over most all time. Individually and collectively, we need to reestablish that role, now. Yet, venturing into the experience is paradoxical. It's a new idea for our culture based on an ancient tradition from most other cultures. Consequently, defining what it means to be a new elder requires us to look both forward and backward simultaneously, to draw from the past while advancing confidently in the direction of the future.

Becoming a New Elder Is Spiritual Work

Much of the everyday literature on aging focuses on health: bodily health first, mental health second. Little is said, though, about what new elders recognize as the critical component: spiritual health. Being a new elder is spiritual work. It is work that acknowledges yet transcends the day-to-day mundane concerns of everyday life and helps forge a connection to something beyond. It involves understanding the temporal in light of the universal. It helps us see our place not just in the world, but in the full universe of possibilities.

As a consequence of this, new elders are easily amused; they see the essential absurdity of it all. Moreover, they have the ability to help others see this absurdity and laugh at things, and themselves, as well.

They see and appreciate the paradoxical nature of life: They realize the more that you know, the less you know; that happiness cannot be pursued directly; that getting love means giving love. They're still growing. They have great curiosity about things and realize they haven't got it all locked up. They accept that there's some stuff they don't know and may never know.

New elders recognize they won't be around forever. Consequently, they have a somewhat paradoxical outlook: On the one hand, they see each moment as precious; on the other hand, they recognize that the time they won't be on Earth is infinitely longer than the time they will be. And so, while they are deeply concerned with the here and now, they are also powerfully in touch with the eternal.

New elders recognize that death is our most profound teacher. Without death, our lives would have no meaning. Death frames an end for us and also puts a value on things. New eldership is, in part, a state of coming to terms with oneself and one's life. It isn't a matter of accepting everything, or of not wishing some things couldn't have been or are not different. But still, it is a matter of accepting things more or less as they are, of realizing that the best that one can do is the best that one can do. New elders don't settle for less than their best efforts, but they do realize that their best efforts may also not achieve the best results. And rather than agonize over what might have been, given how things were, they tend to focus on what may be, given how things are.

One of the most useful practices we have found in the ongoing development that leads to becoming a new elder is to commit one's thoughts to paper in a journal. Journaling allows us to find and express our inner voice in a manner that helps us better understand who we are, where we belong, what we care about, and what our life's purpose is.

The following examples are not meant to be models of the form, but rather, simply to illustrate that if we can do it, so can you.

Richard's Journal Entry

Forget about retiring! I don't like the word retirement. Retirement is a modern invention and my friends in the adult development field are suggesting it may already be obsolete, becoming more rare in the next decade. For me it has come to mean permanent loss of work, a loss of engagement and purpose. I think retirement is a bad idea, anyway. At 59, I established as one of my goals: "to be a productive 80-year-old." As I move through my 60s, I may want to change the pace of my work but not the nature of my work.

At age 70, I see myself casually stretched out in a chair in my Africa-adorned office. On my wall is a quote by T. S. Eliot: "Old men ought to be explorers." And I'm an explorer. Dressed in my trademark black shirt, jeans, and sandals, I'm recounting my thirtieth year of trekking in Africa. At 70, I see myself as a "new elder explorer." I'm exploring a retirement in which age does not matter. In fact, I'm burying the whole notion of retirement. I am a student of and in the process of becoming a "new elder." I see myself just unpacking from a hiking trip in Montana and I'm repacking to speak at an international conference on "The New Elder" in Oslo, Norway, to be followed by a one-month stay in the Bergen, Norway area.

Sally and I "bagged" 30 sleeping-bag nights this year. And this is our goal, 30 nights a year sleeping out—in a tent or without one. At 60, I made a big change. I committed my professional life to studying and living in the radical questions: "What is eldership?" "Who is the new elder?" The field of gerontology and aging has held my interest since my Bush Fellowship in 1973, studying the adult life cycle. Now, as I have become a dedicated student and spokesman for the need for the new elder in society, my work has become increasingly important, not less so. My work now focuses on speaking and writing. I see my vocation now as enlarging the possibility of eldership, not retiring from it. I'm often invited to speak at significant conferences around the world as a model and advocate of the "new elder" in society. Sally and I live a simple, debt-free, uncluttered life. We have a passionate, interdependent partnership based on our shared purposes and our love for each other and for the natural world. My strong voice for the new elder has allowed me to claim a place at the fire. "How do you discover passion?" I'm often asked. "In dreams," I often reply. We all dream in our sleep, but some dream in the daytime.

Passion is not born of vague dreams. My passionate dream is to transform retirement. It is to create a wholly new vision of the new elder in society.

Dave's Journal Entry

I've long had this idea that I will live to be 112 years old. I'm not sure where this notion came from, but I've tried to live my life as if it's true. This has done a couple of things. First, it's made me a bit more patient with my own development. So what if I don't finish my undergraduate degree until I'm 36; I've still got three-quarters of a century to build a career. And big deal if I don't start a family until I'm almost 40; even if my daughter is as slow to get started having kids as I was, I'll still be able to see my grandkids graduate high school.

Second, imagining that I'm going to live to such a ripe old age has completely disabused me of the idea that I'll be able— or even that I would want to—retire at age 65, or even 72. After all, if I'm going to be around for another 60-some years, I'd bet-

ter have something more interesting to do than sitting on the porch, whittling.

Of course, I have no real idea whether I'll live to be 5 score and 12; it's probably fairly unlikely, to tell the truth. Still, I have every intention of continuing to live as if I will. That means that, as I approach 50, I'm only just beginning middle age. I won't be old until I'm in my 90s. It's not as if I'm going to try to remain a kid forever, I'm just going to slow down the process of growing up. My dad had a quote in his office when I was growing up: "We grow too soon old and too late smart." Perhaps I can't do anything about the latter, but I may be able to delay the former. I'll try to keep from being set in my ways; I'll always see myself as a work-in-progress. It will be a long time before I'll accept that it's "too late" to learn something or try something new.

I suppose the danger in this is that I'll never get around to being fully grown. I might keel over and die before I've ever had a chance to retire. To paraphrase The Who, I could die before I get old. Oh well, it could be worse . . . I suppose I could get old before I die.

Growing Whole, Not Old

The primary intent of this chapter is to offer a manifesto in praise of growing whole, not old. This will seem strange only to those unable to recognize the widespread societal antipathy toward growing old. But given the inevitability of the aging process, it's clear any intractable aversion is wrongheaded.

Growing older offers distinctive opportunity for growing whole. If this opportunity should be denied, as it is for many people, both the individual and society as a whole lose. If people in the second half of life are not encouraged to deal with their aging as a vital stage of growth, the rest of us are cut off from wisdom that only the most experienced among us can provide.

Thus, we need a manifesto for growing whole—for bringing forth the wisdom long thought to be a mark of elders. We think of this as a manifesto for the new elder. The dignity inherent in aging is to be seen in the way new elders relate to themselves and the world.

Inevitably, we all have assumptions about how aging is likely to go for us. Most of us tend to have an anachronistic picture of what it means to be elderly. One of the important points we have tried to make in this book, though, is that new elders and elderly are not the same thing.

Through our research and interviews with new elders, we have come to realize that we are living on the boundary between the elderly and the new elder. We need to challenge our outmoded ideas about aging and replace them with bold new ones. Insights are needed and choices must be made.

At the time of the writing of this book, statistics say that, in the United States, 10,000 baby boomers a day are turning 50 years old. That's approximately four million a year for the next 18 years. Two-thirds of all the people who have ever lived past 65 are alive today. Never before in history have so many people entered into this later stage of life so vital, so healthy, and so free. And never before have so many had such a hunger for direction in how to live this stage in a purposeful way.

New elders today have a lot more time to age before they become elderly. With that time, we believe that their biggest personal challenge will be to reinvent themselves for what this longevity could mean.

Carl Jung's observation, "That which youth found and had to find outside of itself, in the second half of life must be found within," rings increasingly true for many people in the second half of life

It's time for a new manifesto for growing whole, not old. This manifesto is illuminated by the four flames of vital aging—principles that can transform the second half of our lives.

Growing whole can free us, personally—and our aging society—to discover a more powerful sense of calling in the second half of life. Becoming a whole new elder can lead to a stage of evolution in our own lives that can also be the key to the evolution and survival of our aging society.

The huge new wave of "seasoned citizens" has to have some function in the survival of the community and our species. It has to go beyond our personal future to the future of the whole. There needs to be a new elder movement that will rekindle the fires necessary for society to productively use the wisdom of age.

Evolution, however, must first come from within. We must claim our place at the fire. Claiming means growing and giving in the elder years of life as whole persons in society. It means using our unique gifts and our stored wisdom to help society move in new, life-affirming directions.

And through our courage, we will create a new elder society. By claiming our place at the fire, we will give voice to what we really think and feel at last. We will move with dignity and presence into that unknown future that we are helping to shape for generations to come.

Here then, is the manifesto by which we will claim our place at the fire.

The Manifesto for New Elders

1. Recall Our Story

We will answer the question "Who Am I?" by recalling our story. Through a review of our lives, recognizing that it is a task of age in itself, not just a legacy for one's grandchildren and heirs, we will come to know ourselves better. The trigger points that make up our lifeline lead us to wholeness of self. They help us to see the totality of our lives and to find the meaning of our life as we have lived it.

2. Refind Our Place

We will answer the question "Where Do I Belong?" by refinding our place. We will allow ourselves to drift and to rediscover our place in the world. We will explore side roads and blue highways. We will postpone the end, postpone criticism. We will disconnect from the clock and let surprising opportunities present themselves. The one irretrievable loss is not living in the moment, and we will endeavor to live with this knowledge in mind.

3. Renew Our Calling

We will answer the "What Do I Care About?" by renewing our calling. We renew our callings by paying attention to what we care about. We will grow along with others who are younger than we are. Growth is different than something that "just happens" to us. We produce it. We live it. The essentials for growth are the openness to experience new situations and the willingness to be changed by them. The moments of connection are what count.

4. Reclaim Our Purpose

We will answer the "What Is My Purpose?" question by reclaiming our purpose. We will reclaim our purpose by acknowledging that it is the mystery of life that keeps us alive. We will let go of our need to control, fix, or even understand everything. We will enjoy the warmth of the fire and spread that warmth around us in new, unexpected, and unexplainable ways. We will claim our place at the fire!

The Best Is Yet To Be

Increasing numbers of psychologists, sociologists, gerontologists, philosophers, and medical researchers have been finding that the commonly held societal patterns of aging and retirement are neither normal nor inevitable. Alternatives exist that we need to seriously consider.

The new elders you met in this book are not exceptions to some supposed general rule of aging. They are individuals who chose to become new elders. They have not bought into the notion that growth and youth are synonymous. All have been discovering hidden callings and initiating creative change. In their 50s, 60s, 70s, and even 80s they have rejected stereotypes of aging and explored new directions.

It is tempting to stay in familiar territory, to tread wellworn tracks and retire from life. The danger is that we could stagnate and miss the opportunity to live on purpose for the second half of our lives.

The exciting news from our interviews with new elders is a story of purpose and possibility. It is an emerging story of new elders who are claiming their place at the fire. Their collective story is one of expanded growth and deepened purpose.

As we face the future, we have a choice. Not everyone believes we have this choice. We do.

We take our cue from the words of Robert Browning's character, Rabbi Ben Ezra: "Grow old along with me! / The best is yet to be,/The last of life, for which the first was made."

 # Notes

xiii: "Do not go gentle into that good night," Dylan Thomas, from *The Poems of Dylan Thomas* (New Directions, 1952).

3: "The first requirement of any society," Joseph Campbell, *The Mythic Dimension: Selected Essays 1958-1987.*

6: "Because it does not know," Ram Dass, *Still Here: Embracing Aging, Changing, and Dying* (Riverhead Books, 2000).

13: "Wholly unprepared, we embark," Carl Jung, *Modern Man in Search of a Soul* (1933).

21: "The call rings up the curtain," Joseph Campbell, *The Hero with a Thousand Faces* (Princeton University Press, 1949).

17: "Life can only be understood backwards," Søren Kierkegaard, *Philosophical Fragments.*

17: T. S. Eliot, "Little Giddings" (1942), © 1969 Valerie Eliot.

20: James Hillman, *The Force of Character: And the Lasting Life* (Ballantine Books, 1999).

21: "Being old is not the same," Betty Friedan, *The Fountain of Age* (Simon & Schuster, 1993).

21: Jane Juska, *A Round-Heeled Woman: My Late-Life Adventures in Sex and Romance* (Villard Books, 2003).

24: Rabbi Zalman Schachter-Shalomi, *From Age-ing to Sage-ing: A Profound New Vision of Growing Older* (Warner Books, 1997).

24: "The thing is to understand myself," Søren Kierkegaard, *Søren Kierkegaard Journal and Papers*, edited by Howard Hong (Indiana University Press, 1976).

25: "It is a great art to saunter," Henry David Thoreau, *Walden* (1854).

30: David Suzuki and Peter Knudtson eds., *Wisdom of the Elders: Sacred Native Stories of Nature* (Bantam, 1992).

34: "When you learn how to die," Mitch Albom, *Tuesdays with Morrie: An Old Man, a Young Man, and Life's Greatest Lesson* (Doubleday, 1997).

35: Great American Think-Off, www.think-off.org

57: "Situations in which we become dependent," Ram Dass, *Still Here: Embracing Aging, Changing, and Dying* (Riverhead Books, 2000).

60: "You cannot step twice," Heraclitus (544-483 BC), *Fragments.*

65: "Imagination is everything," Albert Einstein, *What I Believe* (1933).

71: *About Schmidt* (New Line Cinema Productions, 2002).

78: George E. Vaillant, *Aging Well* (Little Brown, 2002).

100: "Nothing great," Ralph Waldo Emerson, "Circles," in *Ralph Waldo Emerson: Essays and Lectures* (New American Library, 1983).

107: Theodore Roszak, *America the Wise: The Longevity Revolution and the True Wealth of Nations* (Houghton Mifflin, 1998).

107: "I told you to take a leave," Louis Begley, *About Schmidt* (Ballantine Books, 1997).

108: Bill Cosby, *Time Flies* (Doubleday, 1987).

108: Ken Dychtwald, *Age Wave* (Tarcher, 1989).

108: "We live in a strange land," Stephen and Ondrea Levine, *Who Dies: An Investigation of Conscious Living and Conscious Dying* (Anchor Books, 1982).

109: "The real dilemma of existence," Ernest Becker, *The Denial of Death* (Free Press, 1997).

112: "Death is not the enemy," Stephen and Ondrea Levine, *Who Dies.*

116: "Probably in every concentration camp," Viktor E. Frankl, *Man's Search for Meaning: An Introduction to Logotherapy* (Beacon Press, 1962).

118: "Deep self-renewal," Roger L. Gould, *Transformations: Growth and Change in Adult Life* (Simon & Schuster, 1979).

118: Alex Comfort, *Say Yes to Old Age* (Crown, 1990).

120: Alice Seybold, *The Lovely Bones: A Novel* (Little Brown, 2002).

123: "The thing a person's gotta have," John Gardner, *The Art of Living* (Knopf, 1981).

125: "This is the true joy in life," George Bernard Shaw, Epistle dedication to *Man and Superman* (1903).

129: "Every human being," C. G. Jung, *Modern Man in Search of a Soul* (1933).

132: "Old men ought ought to be explorers," T. S. Eliot, "East Coker" (1940).

136: "That which youth found," C. G. Jung, *Modern Man in Search of a Soul* (1933).

139: "Grow old along with me," Robert Browning, "Rabbi Ben Ezra" (1864).

Index

Friedan, Betty, *The Fountain of Age*, 21

Gardner, John, *The Art of Living*, 123
generativity, 77–79
generosity, new elders, 4
gentleness, revolution, 107
gifts, sharing, 115
giving
   away, 105–106, 112
   back, xi
Glenn, John, 16, 65
global positioning systems (GPS), our internal, 52–54
Goethe, 111
Gordon, Ruth, in *Harold and Maude*, 78–79
Gould, Roger, *Transformations*, 118
Gould, Sam, 60–63
Great American Think-Off, 35–36, 88
Great Mid-western Think-Off, 88
growth
   barriers to, 91–93
   catalyst for, 19
   growing whole, not old, 134–136

Habitat for Humanity, xiii–xiv
Hadza
   elders, ix–xv, 50
   fireside experiences, 128
   sense of place, 56
Harold and Maude, 78–79
Heckler, Ricahrd Strozzi, 13–17
help, fundamental need to, 58
Hepburn, Katherine, 85
Heraclitus, 59–60
Hillman, James, *The Force of Character*, 20
home, finding, 50–51
Homer, 92

Honey Guide, The Gift of the, x–xi
hope, elements of, 96–99
Horne, Lena, 65
Hudson, Frederic, 103–106
Hudson Institute, 85–86, 104
hunter-gatherers, villages of, 128
Hutchinson, Betsy, 54–55

ideas, passionate, 89
identity
   age, 85
   flame of, xiv
   recalling our stories, 3, 13–46
   who am I?, 45–46
imagination, vision, 65
immortality, awareness of our, 32–33
International Solidarity Movement (ISM), 83–84
intimacy, community, 3–4
It's a Wonderful Life, 9

Jagger, Mick, 65
Jois, Sri K. Pattabhi, 72–73
journaling, 131
Jung, Carl G., 13–14, 129, 136
Juska, Jane, *A Round-Heeled Woman: My Late-Life Adventures in Sex and Romance*, 21

Kant, 74
Kerrigan, Keith, 58–59
Kierkegaard, Soren
   search for a meaningful life, 24
   understanding life, 17
Knudtson, Peter and David Suzuki, *Wisdom of the Elders*, 30–31
Kubler-Ross, Elizabeth, 109
Larson, Rollie, 109–113

About the Authors

Richard J. Leider is a founding partner of *The Inventure Group*, a coaching and consulting firm in Minneapolis, Minnesota devoted to bringing out the natural potential in people. He is a nationally known writer, speaker, and career coach, and a pioneer in the field of Life/Work Planning. A National Certified Career Coach, he has been helping people to hear and heed their callings for more than 30 years. Author and co-author of five previous books, including the best-sellers *Repacking Your Bags* and *The Power of Purpose*, he is also an online columnist for *Fast Company*.

David A. Shapiro is a writer, philosopher, and educator who finds himself drawn again and again—both personally and professionally—to questions about the meaning and purpose of our lives. David is the Education Director of the Northwest Center for Philosophy for

Children, a nonprofit organization that brings philosophy and philosophers into the lives of students in schools and community forums. He is also an instructor of philosophy at Cascadia Community College, where he works to foster philosophical dialogue among both students and faculty within a postsecondary school setting. David is the author of *Choosing the Right Thing to Do: In Life, at Work, in Relationships, and for the Planet,* and is delighted to have the opportunity to co-create again with his friend and mentor, Richard Leider, with whom he co-authored two other books, *Repacking Your Bags: Lighten Your Load for the Rest of Your Life,* and *Whistle While You Work: Heeding Your Life's Calling.* David lives in Seattle, Washington, with his wife, Jennifer Dixon, and his daughter, Amelia.

Repacking Your Bags
Lighten Your Load for the Rest of Your Life
2nd Edition

Richard J. Leider and David A. Shapiro

Learn how to climb out from under the many burdens you're carrying and find the fulfillment that's missing in your life. A simple yet elegant process teaches you to balance the demands of work, love, and place in order to create and live your own vision of success.

Paperback, 260 pages • ISBN 1-57675-180-5 • Item #51805 $16.95

Whistle While You Work
Heeding Your Life's Calling

Richard J. Leider and David A. Shapiro

We all have have a calling in life. It needs only to be uncovered, not discovered. *Whistle While You Work* makes the uncovering process inspiring and fun. Featuring a unique "Calling Card" exercise—a powerful way to put the whistle in your work—it is a liberating and practical guide that will help you find work that is truly satisfying, deeply fulfilling, and consistent with your deepest values.

Paperback, 200 pages • ISBN 1-57675-103-1 • Item #51031 $16.95

The Power of Purpose
Creating Meaning in Your Life and Work

Richard J. Leider

We all possess a unique ability to do the work we were made for. Concise and easy to read, and including numerous stories of people living on purpose, The Power of Purpose is a remarkable tool to help you find your calling, an original guide to discovering the work you love to do.

Hardcover, 170 pages • ISBN 1-57675-021-3 • Item #50213 $20.00

Audiotape, 2 cassettes, 3 hours • ISBN 1-57453-215-4
Item #32154 $17.95

Berrett-Koehler Publishers
PO Box 565, Williston, VT 05495-9900
Call toll-free! **800-929-2929** 7 am-9 pm EST
Or fax your order to 1-802-864-7626
For fastest service order online: **www.bkconnection.com**

Berrett-Koehler books are available at quantity discounts for orders of 10 or more copies.

Claiming Your Place at the Fire

Living the Second Half of Your Life on Purpose

Richard J. Leider and David A. Shapiro

Paperback original
ISBN 1-57675-297-6
Item #52976 $14.95

To find out about discounts for orders of 10 or more copies for individuals, corporations, institutions, and organizations, please call us toll-free at (800) 929-2929.

To find out about our discount programs for resellers, please contact our Special Sales department at (415) 288-0260; Fax: (415) 362-2512. Or email us at bkpub@bkpub.com.

Subscribe to our free e-newsletter!

To find out about what's happening at Berrett-Koehler and to receive announcements of our new books, special offers, free excerpts, and much more, subscribe to our free monthly e-newsletter at www.bkconnection.com.

Berrett-Koehler Publishers
PO Box 565, Williston, VT 05495-9900
Call toll-free! **800-929-2929** 7 am-9 pm EST
Or fax your order to 1-802-864-7626
For fastest service order online: **www.bkconnection.com**